Unreasonable Doubt

Unreasonable Doubt

How Reason, Science, and History Collapse Without God

SERGIU MARGAN

RESOURCE *Publications* • Eugene, Oregon

UNREASONABLE DOUBT
How Reason, Science, and History Collapse Without God

Copyright © 2025 Sergiu Margan. All rights reserved. Except for brief quotations in critical publications or reviews, no part of this book may be reproduced in any manner without prior written permission from the publisher. Write: Permissions, Wipf and Stock Publishers, 199 W. 8th Ave., Suite 3, Eugene, OR 97401.

Resource Publications
An Imprint of Wipf and Stock Publishers
199 W. 8th Ave., Suite 3
Eugene, OR 97401

www.wipfandstock.com

PAPERBACK ISBN: 979-8-3852-6443-8
HARDCOVER ISBN: 979-8-3852-6444-5
EBOOK ISBN: 979-8-3852-6445-2

VERSION NUMBER 121525

Scripture quotations are taken from The Holy Bible, New International Version®, NIV®. Copyright © 1973, 1978, 1984, 2011 by Biblica, Inc. Used with permission of Zondervan. All rights reserved worldwide. www.zondervan.com.

Contents

Prologue: The Purpose of All Creation | ix

Part 1—The Foundation of Reason
Chapter 1—What Is Logic, and Why It Matters | 3
Chapter 2—Can Something Come from Nothing? | 7
Chapter 3—The Big Bang: Everything from Nothing? | 10
Chapter 4—Consciousness: The Hard Problem That Won't Go Away | 13
Chapter 5—The Moral Law: Why Right and Wrong Point to God | 16
Chapter 6—Justice and Judgment: Why Truth Confronts Us | 19

Part 2—The Voice of God: Testing Revelation and Recognizing Truth
Chapter 1—Has God Spoken? Sifting | 25
Chapter 2—The Center of the Story: Why Everything Points to Jesus | 28
Chapter 3—The Reliability of Scripture: Can We Trust the Record? | 31
Chapter 4—The Human Condition: Why We Need Saving | 34
Chapter 5—The Cross: Where Justice and Mercy Meet | 37
Chapter 6—The Resurrection: The Day Death Lost Its Power | 40
Chapter 7—The Spread of the Gospel: From Jerusalem to the Ends of the Earth | 43
Chapter 8—The Nature of Unbelief and the Cost of Ignoring the Truth | 46

Part 3—The Clash of Worldviews: Why Modern Thinking Cannot Replace God
Chapter 1—The Clash of Worldviews: Why Modern Thinking Cannot Replace God | 51

Chapter 2—Materialism: The Poverty of a World Made Only of Matter | 54
Chapter 3—Relativism: When "Your Truth" Destroys the Truth | 57
Chapter 4—Scientism: When Science Oversteps Its Bounds | 60
Chapter 5—Atheistic Humanism: The Impossible Task of Being Our Own God | 63
Chapter 6—Postmodernism: The Death of Meaning | 66
Chapter 7—Paganism and Pantheism: The Old Gods in New Disguise | 68
Chapter 8—All Religions Are the Same: The Seductive Lie of Spiritual Equality | 70
Chapter 9—The Problem of Evil: How Other Worldviews Avoid the Hardest Question | 74
Chapter 10—The Christian Answer to Suffering and Evil | 77
Chapter 11—The Uniqueness of the Gospel in a World of Competing Truths | 80

Part 4—Standing Firm: Living the Truth in an Age of Deception

Chapter 1—The Age of Deception | 85
Chapter 2—Courage in the Face of the Crowd | 88
Chapter 3—The War for Reality: Truth Under Siege | 91
Chapter 4—When Silence Becomes Complicity | 94
Chapter 5—The Courage to Stand Alone | 97
Chapter 6—Faith Under Fire: Standing True in Trials | 100
Chapter 7—The Cost of Compromise | 103
Chapter 8—Strength in the Secret Place | 106
Chapter 9—The Unshakable Foundation | 109
Chapter 10—When the World Shifts Beneath Your Feet | 112
Chapter 11—Discerning the Spirit of the Age | 115
Chapter 12—Living as Light in the Darkness | 118
Chapter 13—The Reward of Endurance | 121

Part 5—The Global Battlefield of Ideas

Chapter 1—The Global Battlefield of Ideas | 127
Chapter 2—The Great Contenders: How the World Seeks Truth | 132
Chapter 3—Testing the Claims | 136
Chapter 4—Christianity: The Claim and the Proof | 140
Chapter 5—Islam: The Claim and the Challenge | 144
Chapter 6—Hinduism: Hierarchy of Men or the Image of God? | 148

Chapter 7—Buddhism: The Silence of Nirvana vs. the Voice of God | 151
Chapter 8—Judaism: The Root of the Story | 155

Part 6—Deep Philosophical Synthesis
Chapter 1—The Blindness of Modern Genius | 161
Chapter 2—The First Truth: Why Every Story Must Begin with God | 163
Chapter 3—The Architecture of Reality | 165
Chapter 4—The Unity of Truth: From Many Roads to One | 169
Chapter 5—The Law Written on the Heart: Why Morality Points Beyond Evolution | 172
Chapter 6—The Mystery of Consciousness | 176
Chapter 7—The Universal Law: Why Morality Cannot Be Erased | 179
Chapter 8—The Map We Abandoned | 181
Chapter 9—Guardrails Against the Abyss | 185
Chapter 10—The Final Proof: When All Roads Lead to God | 187

Part 7—The Great Convergence
Chapter 1—Where All Truths Meet | 193
Chapter 2—The Timeline That Was Never Chance | 195
Chapter 3—When Every Pursuit Leads to God: The Necessity of Meaning | 197
Chapter 4—The Timeline Revealed | 199
Chapter 5—Justice: The Moral Compass of the Universe | 204
Chapter 6—Knowledge and Beauty: When Truth and Wonder Point Beyond Matter | 208
Chapter 7—The Last Turn Before Home | 212

Part 8—The Unavoidable Decision
Chapter 1—From Convergence to Commitment | 217
Chapter 2—The Courage to Say Yes | 221

Bibliography | 225

Prologue
The Purpose of All Creation

Across the centuries of creation, a mystery has unfolded before witnesses both seen and unseen. We live our lives in flesh and shadow, often unaware that our choices, our pain, and our redemption are the spectacle of the ages—a story not only for us but for the watching hosts of heaven.

Long before humanity walked the earth, the halls of heaven rang with perfect harmony, until the day pride was born in the heart of the brightest angel. Lucifer, adorned with splendor, turned from glory to grasp at the throne. One third of heaven, dazzled by possibility, followed him into the unknown. In that moment, perfection itself cracked, and the universe learned that even the highest can fall. But God did not destroy the rebel. Instead, he allowed the drama to play out upon the stage of time.

The angels must have wondered why. Why did God not end evil with a word? Why did he allow suffering, rebellion, and death to ripple through creation? But in the silence of heaven, a greater wisdom was at work. God would not rule by fear; he would reveal his nature in a way that would leave every being—human or angel—awed forever.

Redemption was not offered to the angels who fell. Their rebellion was total, born in the blinding clarity of God's presence. But when humanity stumbled in darkness, God himself entered the story. He took on flesh, bore our pain, and made a way back for the broken, the doubting, the undeserving.

Prologue

The gospel is not just good news for the lost. It is the lesson heaven never expected: that mercy triumphs over judgment, that love can rise from ashes, and that the lowest can be crowned with glory greater than the highest ever knew.

Through the story of every soul who turns back to God, the universe witnesses a miracle that even angels long to see. Our pain, our perseverance, our repentance, and our transformation are the living proof that God's love cannot be defeated by pride—that his grace can reach deeper than any fall.

No other creature was given this invitation—not the mighty seraphim, not the stars, not the choirs of angels. Only you, a fragile mortal, are called to become a child of God, to carry in yourself the seed of something the heavens marvel to behold.

If you doubt your place in this story, remember: the angels themselves are watching, not in judgment, but in wonder. They see in you the unfolding answer to a mystery older than time, the revelation of a love that stoops lower and lifts higher than any mind could conceive. Your life—however small, however troubled—is the page upon which God writes his greatest truth.

What the angels long to see is not your failure or your struggle, but your becoming. Through you, they witness the nature of God unveiled—the final proof that love, freely chosen, is the mightiest force in creation.

And so, this story begins—not with certainty but with awe. Not with perfection but with hope.

Overview

What you're about to read is not just a critique of modern science—it's a rational journey into the heart of reality.

While the world increasingly trusts scientific theories over faith, this work takes a bold stance: Christianity not only holds its own intellectually—it surpasses modern science in explanatory power, coherence, and evidence.

Here, I invite readers to examine major scientific worldviews—from the big bang and evolution to simulation theory and artificial intelligence—and to uncover their hidden assumptions, logical gaps, and reliance on blind faith. At the same time, I present the Bible not as an outdated relic but as the most complete, consistent, and predictive framework for understanding existence.

The aim is not to dismiss science but to place it in its rightful context. Science can describe aspects of reality, but it cannot explain why there is something rather than nothing, why the laws of physics are so precisely tuned for life, or why moral truths exist at all. Those answers—when examined honestly—point not to randomness or inevitability, but to purpose, intelligence, and a moral lawgiver.

If you approach these pages with an open mind, you may find that faith in God is not a leap into darkness but a step into the clearest light you have ever known. And if you already believe, my hope is that you will leave these pages with a deeper confidence that your faith is not blind—it is the most reasonable conclusion available.

PART 1

The Foundation of Reason

Chapter 1

What Is Logic, and Why It Matters

IMAGINE YOU ARE IN a courtroom. The evidence has been presented, testimony has been provided by witnesses, and the outcome of the verdict is now pending. The decision will change someone's life forever. But instead of weighing the facts, the judge flips a coin.

You would call that unjust. Why?

Because we instinctively know that truth should be discovered, not guessed. And the only reliable way to discover truth is through reasoning—the disciplined process we call logic.

The Nature of Logic

Logic is not a human invention like language or mathematics. It is a framework we discovered—like gravity or the laws of thermodynamics—because it was already there, woven into the fabric of reality. If something is true, it cannot also be false in the same sense at the same time. This is the law of noncontradiction, one of the foundational laws of logic, articulated by Aristotle over two thousand years ago.

We don't create these laws. We uncover them. We cannot vote them out of existence or rewrite them to suit our preferences. They are universal, immaterial, and unchanging. And this raises a crucial question: where do such laws come from?

Why Logic Exists

If the universe is purely physical, everything—including our thoughts—is just the product of atoms colliding in our brains. In that case, "truth" would be whatever our brain chemistry happened to produce, not something objective we could actually know. Yet we live and think as though objective truth exists—and that we can find it.

The existence of logical laws points to something beyond the material. These laws are not made of matter, yet they govern the behavior of matter—and minds. They are eternal, unchanging, and authoritative. In the same way, the God of the Bible is eternal, unchanging, and authoritative. Logic is not above God; it is an expression of his nature.

Historical Witnesses to Logic's Source

From Aristotle to Aquinas to modern philosophers, the consensus is clear: logic is the necessary foundation for all thought and communication. Thomas Aquinas went further, arguing that the very rationality of the universe reflects the mind of its Creator.[1] Even Albert Einstein, who was not a conventionally religious man, marveled that the universe is intelligible at all.[2]

If God does not exist, why should reality follow logical patterns? The atheist can use logic, but they cannot account for its existence without borrowing from a worldview in which reason itself has a rational source.

---

1. Aquinas, *Summa Theologiae*, I/2.3.
2. Einstein, *Out of My Later Years*, 58–94.

What Is Logic, and Why It Matters

The Cost of Abandoning Logic

When a society abandons logic, truth becomes whatever those in power say it is. History is littered with the wreckage of cultures that replaced reason with ideology—from totalitarian regimes to pseudo-scientific movements that justified oppression.

Logic protects us from manipulation. It allows us to challenge false claims, test ideas, and build on knowledge without collapsing into chaos. It is no coincidence that the rise of logic-based reasoning in history—through Greek philosophy and, later, the Christian intellectual tradition—fueled the greatest leaps in science, law, and human rights.

Anticipating the Skeptic

A skeptic might say, "We use logic simply because it works, not because it's divine." But why does it work? Why should the human mind—a product of blind evolutionary processes, according to the skeptic—align perfectly with the deep structure of the universe? The "it just works" answer is not an explanation; it is an evasion.

Why This Matters for You

You use logic every day—when making decisions, solving problems, or recognizing contradictions in what people say. But logic is more than a tool for argument; it is a lifeline to reality. If we can't trust logic, we can't trust anything—not even the belief that logic is untrustworthy.

If logic exists, it points to a rational foundation for reality. And if that foundation is personal—a mind—then that mind is the ultimate source of truth.

Bridge to the Next Chapter

If logic tells us that something cannot come from nothing, then the next question is unavoidable: what does that mean for the origin of the universe? In the next chapter, we confront the claim that nothing can exist before something—and why that is not just improbable but impossible.

Chapter 2

Can Something Come from Nothing?

Picture an empty stage. No actors, no props, no lights—not even the stage itself. Pure nothingness. Now imagine, without cause or reason, a fully scripted play bursting into existence, complete with actors and scenery. It's absurd—yet this is precisely what many claim happened with the universe.

The Impossibility of Absolute Nothing Producing Something

Philosophers and scientists have long recognized that nothing comes from nothing. The law of causality—every effect must have a cause—is not a scientific convention but a foundational truth on which science itself depends. If it were possible for something to come from nothing, then anything could appear at any time, for no reason at all. We do not live in such a chaotic universe.

Some skeptics respond, "Quantum particles appear from nothing all the time." But quantum "nothing" is not absolute nothing. It is a seething ocean of energy governed by physical laws—laws that themselves require explanation. As Alexander Vilenkin notes, even in a "nothing" scenario, the process still presupposes physical law: "The laws of physics must have existed, even though there was no universe."[1]

The Problem of Infinite Regression

If everything needs a cause, what caused the cause? Could there be an infinite chain of causes stretching backward forever? No. An infinite past would mean that today could never arrive. You cannot cross an infinite number of moments to reach the present. Logic demands a starting point.

The Uncaused Cause

This is where the concept of the "uncaused cause"—or the necessary being—comes into play. Something must exist that does not depend on anything else for its existence. This being must be eternal, unchanging, and powerful enough to bring the universe into being. The Bible identifies this cause as God: "In the beginning, God created the heavens and the earth" (Gen 1:1).

Science and the Beginning

Modern cosmology supports a beginning.

The big bang theory, backed by overwhelming evidence, points to a moment when time, space, matter, and energy came into existence. Stephen Hawking admitted, "Almost everyone now believes that the universe, and time itself, had a beginning."[2]

If the universe had a beginning, it cannot be self-existent. Something outside of time and space—something non-physical—must have caused it.

---

1. Vilenkin, *Many Worlds in One*, 181.
2. Hawking et al., *Nature of Space and Time*, 20.

Why This Matters

If the universe is the product of an eternal mind, then everything changes: meaning is possible, purpose is real, and morality is grounded. If not, then we are the byproduct of a cosmic accident, and our search for meaning is futile.

Bridge to the Next Chapter

If the universe had a beginning, then the next question is what kind of universe is it? Is it random and chaotic, or does it bear the unmistakable signature of design?

Chapter 3

The Big Bang
Everything from Nothing?

An explosion is usually a sign of chaos. Yet the so-called "big bang" was no ordinary explosion. It was a precise, finely tuned event that brought forth the laws of physics, the structure of galaxies, and the conditions for life itself.

What the Big Bang Really Means

The big bang theory states that the universe expanded from an unimaginably dense and hot state about 13.8 billion years ago.[1] This was not an explosion into space—space itself began to exist. Before this event, there was no time, no space, no matter.

The Borde-Guth-Vilenkin theorem, one of the most important results in cosmology, shows that any universe that has, on average, been expanding must have a beginning.[2] Even speculative models like the multiverse cannot avoid a cosmic starting point.

---

1. Planck Collaboration, "Planck 2018 Results."
2. Borde et al., "Inflationary Spacetimes."

The Big Bang

The Precision of the Universe

The initial conditions of the universe were set with astonishing precision. The cosmological constant—which controls the expansion of the universe—is fine-tuned to one part in 10^{120}. If it were slightly different, the universe would have either collapsed back into nothingness or expanded so fast that galaxies could never form.

Sir Roger Penrose calculated the odds of our low-entropy universe forming by chance at 1 in $10^{(10^{123})}$.[3] That is a number so large it is effectively impossible to comprehend.

Redefining "Nothing"

Some scientists claim the universe came from "nothing," but in their definition, "nothing" is a quantum vacuum governed by physical laws. This is not philosophical nothingness; it is something. And something requires a cause.

Evidence of Design

The fine-tuning of the universe suggests intentional calibration. The arrangement is so precise that even leading atheist scientists, like Fred Hoyle, have remarked, "A superintellect has monkeyed with physics."[4]

This is consistent with the biblical view: "The heavens declare the glory of God; the skies proclaim the work of his hands" (Ps 19:1).

Why the Big Bang Is a Theological Problem for Atheism

Before the big bang was widely accepted, many atheists argued for a steady-state universe—eternal and self-existing. The big bang

---

3. Penrose, *Road to Reality*, 686–87.
4. Hoyle, "Universe," 12.

shattered that view. If the universe had a beginning, then something—or Someone—beyond it must have caused it.

Bridge to the Next Chapter

If the universe shows evidence of design, then the next question becomes who—or what—is the designer? And why is consciousness central to that answer?

Chapter 4

Consciousness
The Hard Problem That Won't Go Away

You can hold a brain in your hand, but you cannot hold a thought.

Neuroscientists can map brain activity, track chemical signals, and identify which regions fire when you remember your first kiss—yet no scan, no microscope, no machine has ever captured the experience itself. This is the mystery of consciousness: the reality that we are not just biological machines but beings who experience.

The Hard Problem

Philosopher David Chalmers famously called it "the hard problem of consciousness"—the challenge of explaining how subjective experience ("what it's like" to be you) arises from mere matter.[1] Science can tell us how the brain processes information, but it cannot tell us why those processes should give rise to the inner movie of thoughts, sensations, and emotions.

---

1. Chalmers, "Facing Up to the Problem," 200–202.

If we are nothing more than physical matter, then our sense of "self" is an illusion. But if that were true, the illusion would be no one's illusion—because there would be no "you" to have it.

The Failure of Materialism

Materialist explanations reduce consciousness to neural firing patterns. But this is like saying the meaning of a book is nothing but ink on paper. The ink matters—but so does the story it conveys, and that story is not reducible to its physical medium.

John Searle, a philosopher who is not a Christian, notes that consciousness remains a major explanatory challenge: "How is such a thing possible at all? How could the brain cause consciousness? In current discussions this is often called the 'hard problem' and the lack of an explanation of how the brain does it is called the 'explanatory gap.'"[2]

Consciousness and the Image of God

The Bible presents humans as uniquely made in the image of God (Gen 1:27). This "image" includes self-awareness, moral reasoning, creativity, and the ability to love—all hallmarks of consciousness. These traits are not accidental byproducts of evolution; they are fingerprints of a Mind that made us.

Near-Death Experiences and Evidence Beyond the Brain

Accounts of people who have been clinically dead—without measurable brain activity—yet report vivid experiences, challenge the idea that consciousness is produced solely by the brain. While such reports are controversial, their consistency across cultures and the inability of brain-only models to explain them are striking.

---

2. Searle, *Mind*, 40.

The Logic of Mind from Mind

If consciousness exists, it must come from a source capable of consciousness. You cannot get awareness from unawareness any more than you can get language from rocks. The most coherent explanation is that our minds come from a greater Mind—one that is eternal, self-existent, and personal.

Why This Matters

If we are nothing more than matter, then love, beauty, and morality are just chemical side effects. But if we are conscious souls, then our lives have meaning that transcends biology. The choices we make are not mere survival strategies; they are moral acts that matter in eternity.

Bridge to the Next Chapter

If our very awareness points to a conscious Creator, then the next step is to ask what kind of morality flows from that Creator. Is morality just cultural preference, or is it a code written into the fabric of reality?

Chapter 5

The Moral Law
Why Right and Wrong Point to God

If you found a wallet full of cash on the street, what would you do? Your answer says something about more than just your upbringing—it reveals whether you believe morality is real or merely an illusion.

The Reality of Moral Experience

Most people, no matter their culture, recognize certain things as wrong: torturing children for fun, betraying a friend, murdering the innocent. This is what C. S. Lewis called the "Tao"—the universal moral law embedded in humanity.[1] Even when we disagree on details, we appeal to an unseen standard we expect others to recognize.

If morality were purely a product of evolution or culture, then it would have no ultimate authority. Killing might be wrong in one society and acceptable in another—and neither would be objectively right or wrong. Yet our moral outrage at genocide or slavery suggests we believe in a higher standard that transcends human opinion.

1. Lewis, "Men Without Chests," in *Abolition of Man*.

Morality and the Problem for Atheism

If there is no God, moral laws are just social conventions—useful for survival, perhaps, but ultimately arbitrary. As atheist philosopher Jean-Paul Sartre admitted, without God there can be no objective values.[2] This leads to a troubling conclusion: without God, no action—not even the worst atrocities—is truly wrong in an ultimate sense.

The Source of the Moral Law

Moral laws are not physical laws like gravity; they cannot be measured with instruments. Yet they bind us just as firmly. If they are not the product of human invention, they must come from beyond humanity. The best explanation is that they are rooted in the character of a moral Lawgiver.

In the Bible, morality is not arbitrary commands from a cosmic dictator. God's moral law reflects his nature: his goodness, justice, and love. This is why murder is wrong: it violates the image of God in others. This is why lying is wrong: it contradicts the God who is truth.

The Moral Argument for God

1. If God does not exist, objective moral values and duties do not exist.
2. Objective moral values and duties do exist.
3. Therefore, God exists.

This simple argument is one of the most powerful in philosophy. It is not enough to say "people believe in morality"—the question is, why should morality exist at all in a godless universe?

---

2. Sartre, *Existentialism Is a Humanism*.

When Morality Is Ignored

History shows what happens when societies abandon objective morality. Nazi Germany, Stalinist Russia, and Mao's China all rejected divine moral authority—and left a trail of mass graves. When morality is untethered from God, power becomes the only measure of right and wrong.

Why This Matters

If morality is real, then it points beyond itself to a moral Source. That means our choices are not trivial—they are eternally significant. Every act of kindness echoes God's character; every act of cruelty denies it.

Bridge to the Next Chapter

If morality reflects the character of God, then justice is not an abstract ideal but a personal reality. And if God is just, then judgment is not optional—it is inevitable.

Chapter 6

Justice and Judgment
Why Truth Confronts Us

We like the idea of justice—until it turns its gaze on us.

We cheer when criminals are caught, when tyrants are overthrown, when corruption is exposed. But if every deed, word, and thought of our own lives were brought into the light, would we feel the same way? The idea of divine justice forces us to face not just the evil in the world but the evil within ourselves.

The Universal Cry for Justice

Across cultures and centuries, humans have longed for justice. Myths, laws, and revolutions are built on the conviction that wrongs must be righted. Even atheists cry out against injustice—revealing that justice is not a religious construct but a moral reality embedded in human nature.

Yet perfect justice is elusive in human courts. Criminals walk free. The innocent suffer. History is littered with unfinished cases. The longing for justice that transcends time and circumstance points to a Judge who cannot be bribed, deceived, or overpowered.

God as the Perfect Judge

The Bible describes God as "a righteous judge" (Ps 7:11) who "will by no means clear the guilty" (Exod 34:7). His justice is not like human justice, prone to error or bias. He knows every fact, every motive, every hidden act. This makes his verdicts inescapably accurate—and terrifying for the guilty.

The Problem of Mercy

If God is perfectly just, how can he also be merciful? Justice demands payment for wrongdoing; mercy offers forgiveness. These seem like opposites—until we see the cross. In Jesus, justice and mercy meet. Sin is punished, but the punishment is borne by the innocent on behalf of the guilty.

This is not a loophole in justice—it is justice fulfilled. Every wrong is accounted for, either by being paid for at the cross or by the wrongdoer in final judgment.

Judgment as a Good Thing

We often think of judgment as purely negative, but in Scripture, judgment is also about setting things right. For the oppressed, God's judgment is liberation. For the faithful, it is vindication. For the corrupt, it is exposure. Without judgment, evil would have the last word.

Why Avoiding Judgment Fails

Some avoid the thought of judgment by denying God's existence. But disbelief is not a defense; it is a gamble. If God exists and is just, then justice will be done whether or not we prepare for it.

The Urgency of Truth

If judgment is real, then truth matters now.

Every moral choice, every belief, every rejection or acceptance of God's offer will be weighed. This is why the gospel is urgent: it is not just an invitation to a better life but a summons to be ready for the day when justice will be perfect and final.

Bridge to Part 2

If truth and justice are ultimate realities, then the next question is, has God spoken? And if he has, where can we find his voice among the competing claims of religion, philosophy, and science?

PART 2

The Voice of God

Testing Revelation and Recognizing Truth

Chapter 1

Has God Spoken?
Sifting

Truth from the Noise of the World

If truth matters—and if justice is inevitable—the next question is unavoidable: has God spoken? And if so, how would we recognize his voice among the thousands of religious, philosophical, and ideological claims competing for our allegiance?

The Human Hunger for Revelation

From ancient temples to modern TED Talks, humanity has always sought answers to the ultimate questions: Who are we? Why are we here? What happens when we die? This longing is universal, and it suggests that we are wired for meaning. Yet the sheer variety of answers is overwhelming—from the polytheism of antiquity to the secular humanism of today.

Not all claims to truth are equal. Some can be tested historically. Others collapse under logical scrutiny. If God exists, and if he cares about justice and truth, then it is reasonable to expect that he would reveal himself in a way that is both clear and consistent.

The Test of Coherence

A true revelation from God must be logically coherent. It cannot contradict itself or deny reality as we experience it. A message from the Creator of logic will not violate the laws of logic.

This immediately disqualifies systems that rely on circular reasoning, internal contradictions, or unverifiable myths.

The Test of Evidence

If God has spoken in history, there should be evidence—real events, real places, real people. The Bible anchors its claims in history: the exodus, the reign of kings, the crucifixion and resurrection of Jesus. These are not vague moral stories but testable historical claims. By contrast, many religious texts are set in timeless, placeless realms that resist verification.

The Test of Transformation

A true revelation must have the power to transform lives for good, consistently, across cultures and centuries. The message of Jesus has done precisely this: producing societies that value human dignity, inspiring movements for justice, and giving hope to the hopeless. False revelations may inspire fervor, but they ultimately leave moral and spiritual ruin in their wake.

Competing Voices

In our age, the noise is deafening: secular ideologies promising liberation through self-definition; new spiritual movements offering mystical experiences without moral accountability; ancient religions revived in modern packaging. Each claims to hold the truth, yet their messages often contradict both each other and the reality of the human condition.

Why the Bible Stands Apart

The Bible does not merely claim to be the word of God—it invites scrutiny. Its prophecies have been fulfilled with precision. Its historical details align with archaeology. Its moral vision is both lofty and livable, rooted in the character of a God who is both just and merciful. And unlike philosophies that leave salvation in human hands, the Bible offers grace—the undeserved favor of God—as the foundation for redemption.

The Stakes

If God has spoken, ignoring his word is not a neutral act; it is a rejection of truth itself. The question is not simply academic. Our response will shape our lives, our moral compass, and our eternal destiny.

Bridge to the Next Chapter

If the Bible is the reliable record of God's voice, then the next question is: who is at the center of its message, and why does everything hinge on him?

Chapter 2

The Center of the Story
Why Everything Points to Jesus

If the Bible is the record of God's voice in history, then its central theme is not law, prophecy, or moral instruction—it is a person. From Genesis to Revelation, the narrative bends toward one figure: Jesus Christ.

The Thread Running Through Scripture

The Old Testament lays the foundation, weaving promises and prophecies into the history of Israel. The law reveals humanity's inability to meet God's standard. The prophets speak of a coming King, a suffering Servant, a Redeemer who will bear the sins of many. Every story, from the ark of Noah to the throne of David, points forward to him.

The New Testament unveils him as the fulfillment of every promise. The Gospels record his life, death, and resurrection. Acts tells of his Spirit at work in the church. The epistles explain the meaning of his work. Revelation shows his ultimate triumph.

Why Jesus Is Unique

Religious founders often claim to point the way to God. Jesus claimed to be the way. "I am the way and the truth and the life," he said (John 14:6). This is not the language of a mere prophet or moral teacher—it is the claim of someone who identifies himself with the divine.

He is also unique in that his identity is bound to verifiable history. He lived under Roman rule, in a known place and time. His execution is recorded not only in Scripture but in Roman and Jewish sources.[1] His resurrection was proclaimed in the very city where he was crucified, within weeks of his death[2]—something impossible if the tomb had not been empty.

The Fulfillment of Prophecy

Jesus fulfilled dozens of Old Testament prophecies with precision: his birthplace in Bethlehem (Mic 5:2), his lineage from David (Jer 23:5), his rejection and suffering (Isa 53), his death by crucifixion (Ps 22), and even the timing of his arrival (Dan 9). The statistical probability of one person fulfilling these by chance is astronomical.

The Intersection of Justice and Mercy

In Jesus, justice and mercy converge. The cross is where the penalty for sin is fully paid, and where grace is freely offered. This is why the gospel is not merely advice for a better life—it is the announcement that salvation has been accomplished.

Why Everything Hinges on Him

Remove Jesus from Christianity and nothing remains. Without his resurrection, the apostles would have been liars, the church a

---

1. Tacitus, *Annals* 15.44; Josephus, *Jewish Antiquities* 18.3.3, 20.9.1; Babylonian Talmud, San. 43a.

2. 1 Cor 15:3–7; Acts 2–4; Josephus, *Jewish Antiquities* 18.3.3.

fraud, and the gospel an empty promise. The apostle Paul said it plainly: "If Christ has not been raised, your faith is futile; you are still in your sins" (1 Cor 15:17).

The Invitation

If Jesus is who he claimed to be, then every human being faces a choice: to follow him or to reject him. There is no neutral ground. His claims demand a verdict.

Bridge to the Next Chapter

If Jesus is the center of God's revelation, then the next step is to examine the reliability of the documents that tell his story—the Scriptures themselves.

Chapter 3

The Reliability of Scripture
Can We Trust the Record?

If Jesus is the center of the story, the next question is unavoidable: how do we know the story we have today is the one originally told? The reliability of Scripture is not a side issue. If the documents that record God's revelation have been corrupted or fabricated, then the foundation of faith crumbles.

Manuscript Evidence

No other ancient document is as well-attested as the Bible. The New Testament alone has over 5,800 Greek manuscripts, some dating to within decades of the original writings.[1] In comparison, works of classical antiquity—like those of Plato or Caesar—survive in a handful of manuscripts, often separated from the originals by centuries.[2]

The Dead Sea Scrolls, discovered in the mid-twentieth century, confirmed the remarkable preservation of the Old Testament.

---

1. Metzger and Ehrman, *Text of the New Testament*, 52–53; Ehrman and Wallace, "Textual Reliability."
2. Bruce, *New Testament Documents*; McDowell, *Evidence That Demands a Verdict*.

Texts copied more than a thousand years apart matched with astonishing accuracy, demonstrating that the Scriptures were transmitted with care and reverence.[3]

Archaeological Confirmation

Time and again, archaeology has vindicated the Bible's historical claims. The existence of King David, once doubted, was confirmed by the Tel Dan Stele.[4] The Pool of Siloam, where Jesus healed a blind man, was uncovered in Jerusalem.[5] Even minor details—like place names and political titles—have been shown to align with historical evidence.

Internal Consistency

Written over a span of 1,500 years by more than forty authors from diverse backgrounds, the Bible presents a unified story from creation to redemption. Its moral vision and theological themes remain consistent throughout, pointing to a single divine Author behind the human writers.

Addressing the Charge of Corruption

Some claim that the Bible has been altered over time to suit the needs of the church or political powers. Yet the sheer volume of manuscripts—in multiple languages and scattered across continents—makes such coordinated alteration impossible. Variations that do exist are almost entirely minor spelling differences or word order changes; none affecting the core message.

---

3. Archer, *Survey of Old Testament Introduction*, 23–25; Bruce, *Books and the Parchments*, 118–120.

4. Biran and Naveh, "An Aramaic Stele Fragment"; Biran and Naveh, "Tel Dan Inscription."

5. Shanks, "Pool of Siloam."

The Stakes of Trust

If Scripture is reliable, then its claims about Jesus, salvation, and God's nature stand with authority. If it is not, then Christianity is reduced to speculation and sentiment. The credibility of the Bible is the credibility of the gospel itself.

Why This Matters for Reason

Skeptics often demand evidence for faith. The preservation, corroboration, and consistency of the Bible provide precisely that. Faith is not belief without evidence—it is trust built on the evidence of God's actions in history.

Bridge to the Next Chapter

If the Scriptures are trustworthy, then we can examine their central claims about the human condition—and why we need the salvation they describe.

Chapter 4

The Human Condition
Why We Need Saving

The Bible does more than tell the story of God; it tells the story of us—and it does so with unsettling honesty. From the first pages of Genesis to the last words of Revelation, Scripture's assessment of humanity is consistent: we are created in the image of God, yet deeply corrupted by sin.

The Diagnosis

Sin is more than wrongdoing; it is a state of the heart. The prophet Jeremiah wrote, "The heart is deceitful above all things and beyond cure. Who can understand it?" (Jer 17:9). This is not pessimism; it is realism. Even our best actions can be tainted by selfish motives, pride, or the desire for recognition.

The Universality of Moral Failure

The apostle Paul declared, "All have sinned and fall short of the glory of God" (Rom 3:23). Across cultures and centuries, humanity has been unable to live up to its own moral standards, let alone God's perfect standard. History is littered with empires, movements, and ideologies that promised to fix human nature, only to collapse under the weight of their own corruption.

The Limits of Human Effort

Modern society often frames moral failure as a lack of education, opportunity, or social reform. While these factors matter, they cannot change the human heart. Technology can make life easier, but it cannot make us better. Laws can restrain evil, but they cannot erase the desire to do wrong.

Sin vs. Flaws

Secular thinking tends to reduce sin to "mistakes" or "imperfections"—weaknesses that can be overcome with enough willpower or therapy. The Bible presents a deeper problem: we are not simply people who make bad choices; we are people whose nature is inclined toward rebellion against God. This rebellion is not merely breaking rules; it is rejecting relationship with the One who made us.

The Consequences

The Bible teaches that the result of sin is death—not just physical death but spiritual separation from God. Left to ourselves, we cannot bridge the gap. Our need is not for self-improvement but for rescue.

Preparing for the Gospel

This is why the gospel is not just "good advice" but "good news." It does not tell us how to climb up to God; it tells us that God came down to us. Only by understanding the depth of our need can we grasp the magnitude of his grace.

Bridge to the Next Chapter

If the human condition is as desperate as Scripture says, then the question becomes, what has God done to address it? The answer lies at the cross.

Chapter 5

The Cross
Where Justice and Mercy Meet

THE CROSS STANDS AT the center of history. It is not merely a symbol of faith; it is the place where the full weight of God's justice and the full depth of his mercy meet in a single moment. Without the cross, the gospel is reduced to good intentions. With it, the gospel becomes the power of God to save.

The Problem Only God Could Solve

If God is just, he must punish sin. If he is merciful, he must forgive. But how can both be true without compromising one or the other? Human systems of justice can show mercy, but often at the expense of justice. The cross is the divine solution: God himself bears the penalty his justice demands so that his mercy can be freely given.

The Willing Sacrifice

Jesus was not an unwilling victim of divine wrath. He said, "No one takes my life from me, but I lay it down of my own accord" (John 10:18). The cross was not divine child abuse; it was the self-offering of the Son, fully God and fully man, in perfect unity with the Father's will.

The Depth of the Cost

Crucifixion was designed to inflict maximum pain and humiliation. Yet the physical agony was not the greatest suffering Jesus endured. On the cross, he bore the weight of humanity's sin, experiencing the separation from the Father that sin produces. In that moment, he drank the cup of judgment to its last drop.

The Great Exchange

At the heart of the cross is substitution: "God made him who had no sin to be sin for us, so that in him we might become the righteousness of God" (2 Cor 5:21). Our guilt was placed on him; his righteousness is placed on us. This is not a transaction we earn—it is a gift we receive.

Answering the Critics

Some argue that the cross is unnecessary, that God could simply forgive without sacrifice. But this ignores the reality that forgiveness without justice is not moral; it is moral indifference. The cross proclaims that God takes sin seriously—so seriously that he would rather bear its penalty himself than leave us condemned.

The Universal Invitation

The cross is not limited by culture, race, or era. It speaks to the oppressed and the oppressor, the rich and the poor, the skeptic and the seeker. At the foot of the cross, all stand on level ground. Forgiveness is offered to all who will receive it.

Bridge to the Next Chapter

If the cross is where the penalty was paid, the resurrection is where the victory was secured. Without the resurrection, the cross would be a noble tragedy; with it, the cross becomes the doorway to life.

Chapter 6

The Resurrection
The Day Death Lost Its Power

The resurrection of Jesus is not an optional belief for Christians; it is the hinge upon which the entire faith turns. Without it, the cross would be a noble act of sacrifice but, ultimately, a defeat. With it, the cross becomes the victory over sin, death, and hell.

The Claim That Changed History

On the third day after his crucifixion, Jesus' tomb was found empty. His followers claimed to have seen him alive, not as a vision or a memory, but in physical, tangible form. They ate with him, touched him, and spoke with him. These claims were made in Jerusalem—the very city where he had been executed—when anyone could have checked the tomb.

The Historical Evidence

The empty tomb is supported by multiple lines of evidence. It was discovered by women, whose testimony in the first-century Jewish culture carried little weight—a detail unlikely to be invented by early Christians seeking credibility. The earliest written records of the resurrection date to within a few years of the event,[1] far too soon for legend to replace fact.

Post-resurrection appearances were reported by individuals, small groups, and even over five hundred people at once (1 Cor 15:6). These encounters transformed frightened disciples into bold witnesses, willing to die for their testimony.

Why Alternative Theories Fail

Some suggest that the disciples stole the body. But this fails to explain their willingness to suffer and die for what they knew would be a lie. Others claim the appearances were hallucinations, but hallucinations are individual, not shared by groups—and they do not explain the empty tomb. The idea that Jesus merely fainted and revived is equally implausible, given the severity of Roman execution methods.

The Power of the Resurrection

The resurrection is not just a historical claim; it is a present reality. It declares that death is not the end, that the grave does not have the final word, and that Jesus has authority over life itself. It is the guarantee that his promises are true and that those who belong to him will also rise.

The Cornerstone of Hope

The apostle Paul wrote, "If Christ has not been raised, your faith is futile; you are still in your sins" (1 Cor 15:17). The resurrection is not merely evidence of God's power—it is the assurance that sin's debt has been paid in full, and that eternal life is secured.

---

1. Dunn, *Jesus Remembered*, 855–56; Habermas, "1 Corinthians 15:3–7."

Bridge to the Next Chapter

The resurrection did more than change theology; it ignited a movement. The same men and women who had fled in fear became unstoppable witnesses. The next chapter will explore how the gospel spread from Jerusalem to the ends of the earth.

Chapter 7

The Spread of the Gospel
From Jerusalem to the Ends of the Earth

THE RESURRECTION WAS NOT the end of the story; it was the beginning of a movement that would outlive empires and redefine history. The gospel did not spread because of political power, military force, or economic influence. It spread because the truth cannot be buried—and because those who had seen the risen Christ could not remain silent.

From Fear to Fearlessness

Before the resurrection, the disciples were hiding behind locked doors, afraid of the same authorities who had crucified their Master. After the resurrection, they stood in public squares, proclaiming the gospel with boldness, knowing it would cost them their lives. Peter, who had denied Jesus three times, now confronted the very leaders who condemned him, declaring that salvation is found in no one else.

The Perfect Moment in History

The spread of the gospel happened in what historians call the "fullness of time" (Gal 4:4).[1] The Roman Empire provided a vast network of roads and a common language (Koine Greek), making travel and communication possible on an unprecedented scale.[2] The *Pax Romana*—Roman peace—allowed the message to cross borders without the constant threat of war.[3]

A Message That Could Be Tested

The gospel began in Jerusalem, the very place where Jesus had been crucified and buried. If the resurrection were a lie, it could have been easily disproven within days. Instead, thousands in that city came to believe, many of whom had witnessed the events firsthand. Christianity's explosive growth was rooted in verifiable claims, not secret revelations.

The Power of Persecution

Far from extinguishing the gospel, persecution became its catalyst. As believers fled from hostile authorities, they carried the message with them into new cities and regions. The blood of the martyrs became the seed of the church. Rome's attempts to crush Christianity only revealed its inability to destroy the truth.

Transforming the World

Within a few centuries, the gospel had reached the heart of the empire that once sought to erase it. Slavery, infanticide, and the devaluation of human life—common in the ancient world—were challenged and ultimately transformed by the Christian vision of human dignity.

1. Bruce, *New Testament Documents*, 17–19.
2. Wright, *Jesus and the Victory of God*, 37–39.
3. Blomberg, *Historical Reliability of the Gospels*, 49–52.

The Unstoppable Nature of Truth

The spread of the gospel is not merely a chapter in history; it is evidence of God's hand in history.

No political force, no cultural resistance, no philosophical system has been able to erase it. Empires have risen and fallen, but the message of Jesus Christ continues to circle the globe.

Bridge to the Next Chapter

The spread of the gospel is proof that God's plan is advancing. But the question remains: if the message is true, why do so many still reject it? The next chapter will explore the nature of unbelief—and the cost of ignoring the truth.

Chapter 8

The Nature of Unbelief and the Cost of Ignoring the Truth

Unbelief is rarely a matter of lacking evidence; more often, it is a matter of refusing it. The human heart is not a neutral judge weighing facts in a vacuum. It is a throne—and whoever sits upon it rules the life. For many, the greatest barrier to belief is not the mind but the will.

Seeing but Not Seeing

In the gospels, the Pharisees witnessed miracles, heard Jesus teach with authority, and yet plotted his death. Their problem was not ignorance; it was the unwillingness to surrender their authority, status, and control. They saw the light but closed their eyes.

The Role of Pride

Pride is the root of unbelief. To accept the truth of God is to admit that we are not self-sufficient, that we are not the final authority on right and wrong. For those who have built their identity on self-rule, this is a death too great to contemplate. The gospel demands humility—and pride resists it with all its strength.

The Nature of Unbelief and the Cost of Ignoring the Truth

Moral Resistance

Jesus said, "Light has come into the world, but people loved darkness instead of light because their deeds were evil" (John 3:19). Belief in God carries moral implications. If God is real, then his commands are binding. For some, rejecting God is not about doubting his existence but about rejecting his right to rule.

The Illusion of Neutrality

Many claim to be "open-minded" seekers, but no one approaches the question of God without bias. Our presuppositions, experiences, and desires all shape how we interpret evidence. True seeking requires the courage to let the truth inconvenience us.

The Eternal Stakes

Ignoring the truth of God is not like ignoring a weather forecast. The stakes are eternal. Jesus spoke of a day when every person will give an account. To reject him now is to choose separation from Him forever. Unbelief is not simply a personal choice; it is a cosmic one, aligning oneself against the Author of life.

The Cost of Delay

Some intend to believe later, when life is calmer or questions feel less pressing. But the longer the heart resists, the harder it becomes to yield. Faith is not merely an intellectual conclusion; it is a response to God's call in the present.

Bridge to Part 3

We have seen why the gospel is true and why it spread, but also why many reject it. In the next part, we will confront the competing worldviews of our age—and see how they collapse without God.

PART 3

The Clash of Worldviews
Why Modern Thinking Cannot Replace God

Chapter 1

The Clash of Worldviews
Why Modern Thinking Cannot Replace God

EVERY GENERATION TELLS ITSELF a story about what is real, what is true, and what is worth living for. Our age is no different—except in one crucial way: we have convinced ourselves that we no longer need God in the story.

From classrooms to courtrooms, media to politics, the dominant voices of our time insist that faith belongs to the past. Science, technology, and human reason—we are told—can explain everything worth knowing and solve every problem worth solving. The implication is clear: God is either irrelevant, imaginary, or worse, an obstacle to progress.

The New Religion of the Self

Modern culture has not removed worship from human life; it has simply replaced the object of worship.

The altar is now the self. Our highest authority is personal preference. Our greatest moral command is "be true to yourself." But a self without God is a self without an anchor—adrift on a sea of shifting desires.

The Hidden Assumptions of Secularism

Secularism claims to be neutral, but it smuggles in its own beliefs: that matter is all that exists, that morality can be built without transcendence, and that humanity can define its own meaning. These assumptions are not proven; they are taken on faith. And when tested, they collapse.

The Fragility of a Godless Morality

Without God, morality becomes a matter of consensus or convenience. What is "right" today can be "wrong" tomorrow if the majority decides it so. History shows that human consensus has justified slavery, genocide, and oppression. Without an unchanging standard above us, morality bends to the will of the powerful.

Science Without God

Science is one of humanity's greatest achievements—but it cannot replace God. It can describe how things work but not why they exist. It can extend life but not explain its ultimate purpose. When science is asked to answer questions it was never designed to address, it ceases to be science and becomes ideology.

The Cost of Excluding God

The experiment of building a world without God is not theoretical. The last century saw ideologies rooted in atheism—from Soviet communism to Nazi Germany—produce death on a scale the world had never seen. When human power is absolute and unaccountable to any higher law, the result is tyranny.

Bridge to the Next Chapter

The modern world is full of competing worldviews that promise truth, freedom, and fulfillment. But when measured against reality, they crumble. In the next chapter, we will examine materialism—the belief that only the physical world exists—and see why it cannot bear the weight of human experience.

Chapter 2

Materialism
The Poverty of a World Made Only of Matter

Materialism claims that reality is nothing more than the physical universe—atoms in motion, governed by impersonal laws. According to this view, everything we see, feel, think, or believe is ultimately the product of matter interacting with matter. There is no soul, no spirit, no God—only particles and the forces that push them.

It is a worldview that promises clarity but delivers emptiness.

The Core Assumption

Materialism begins with the assumption that what cannot be measured does not exist. This is not a scientific conclusion but a philosophical one. Science itself cannot prove that only physical things exist; it must take that as a belief. In this way, materialism hides its own faith—a faith that denies anything beyond the reach of its instruments.

The Collapse of Morality

If materialism is true, morality is nothing more than chemical reactions in the brain, shaped by evolution to help us survive. Right and wrong become illusions—survival strategies dressed up in moral language. But if morality is an illusion, then justice is an illusion. Love is an illusion. Even the grief we feel at the loss of someone we love is just neurons firing in response to a stimulus.

This is not how we live. We know, deep in our bones, that love is more than chemistry and that justice is more than social convenience.

The Self-Refuting Nature of Materialism

If our thoughts are the product of blind physical processes, then they are not aimed at truth but at survival. Why should we trust the reasoning of a brain evolved only to pass on genes? Under strict materialism, even the belief in materialism is just a byproduct of neurons firing—no more "true" than any superstition.

In earlier chapters, we saw that truth is not a human invention but a reflection of God's nature. Materialism cuts itself off from this source of truth, and in doing so, undercuts its own credibility.

Science Needs the Immaterial

Materialism often claims the authority of science, yet science itself rests on realities that are not material: the laws of logic, the reality of numbers, the reliability of memory, the trustworthiness of our senses. These cannot be weighed, touched, or measured—yet without them, science collapses.

The Poverty of a Godless Universe

A world of nothing but matter cannot offer meaning, purpose, or hope. The universe does not care about justice. It will not remember you. In a purely material cosmos, every life ends in the same silence, and every achievement is eventually swallowed by entropy.

But we have seen—through the resurrection, through the spread of the gospel, through the moral law written on our hearts—that this is not the kind of universe we inhabit. We live in a creation filled with meaning, governed by moral order, and sustained by the God who made us.

Bridge to the Next Chapter

If materialism denies the existence of ultimate truth, relativism denies that truth can be known at all. The next chapter will expose why "your truth" and "my truth" cannot coexist without collapsing into chaos.

Chapter 3

Relativism

When "Your Truth" Destroys the Truth

RELATIVISM IS THE BELIEF that truth is not absolute but varies from person to person or culture to culture. In its popular form, it sounds appealing: "What's true for you may not be true for me." It promises tolerance, humility, and freedom. But in reality, it delivers confusion, contradiction, and the slow erosion of meaning.

The Self-Contradiction at Its Core

The moment someone says, "There is no absolute truth," they have made an absolute truth claim. Relativism cannot stand without undermining itself. If all truth is relative, then so is the claim that all truth is relative—and it collapses under its own weight.

The Disappearance of Justice

If truth is whatever we want it to be, justice becomes impossible. Imagine a court where the accused says, "In my truth, I am innocent," and the victim says, "In my truth, he is guilty." Without an objective standard, both are equally valid—and equally meaningless.

History shows that the most oppressive regimes thrive in environments where truth is malleable. When the definition of reality can be rewritten at will, the powerful dictate "truth" to serve their interests.

From Tolerance to Tyranny

Relativism presents itself as the champion of tolerance, but it cannot tolerate those who believe in absolute truth. The moment you claim that something is universally right or wrong, relativism brands you as intolerant. It silences dissent in the name of diversity.

This is the same dynamic we saw in earlier chapters when pride refuses correction and unbelief rejects God's authority. Relativism is simply pride dressed in polite, philosophical clothing.

Truth and Freedom

Jesus said, "You will know the truth, and the truth will set you free" (John 8:32).

Freedom is not found in escaping truth but in living within it. A pilot is free to fly only when he obeys the laws of aerodynamics; a society is free only when it aligns itself with the moral and spiritual laws of its Creator.

The God-Shaped Standard

Without God, truth becomes whatever the majority says it is—or whatever the most powerful can impose. With God, truth is anchored beyond human opinion, unshakable and eternal. This is why relativism must ultimately give way to revelation.

Bridge to the Next Chapter

Relativism denies that we can know truth; scientism claims that science alone can give it to us. In the next chapter, we will see why scientism is not science—and why it cannot answer the deepest questions of human existence.

Chapter 4

Scientism
When Science Oversteps Its Bounds

Science is one of humanity's greatest achievements. It has cured diseases, mapped the stars, and unlocked the secrets of DNA. But there is a growing belief—called scientism—that science is not only the best way to know truth but the only way. This belief is not science; it is philosophy masquerading as science.

The Difference Between Science and Scientism

Science is a method—a disciplined way of observing the world, forming hypotheses, and testing them through experimentation. Scientism, by contrast, is the claim that nothing can be known outside of what science can measure. This is a philosophical claim that science itself cannot prove.

To say "only science can give us truth" is to make a statement that cannot be tested scientifically. It is self-refuting, like relativism. It assumes what it cannot demonstrate.

The Limits of Science

Science can describe how a process works, but it cannot tell us why it exists. It can explain the chemical processes of love, but it cannot explain why love matters. It can measure the effects of morality, but it cannot define what is right and wrong. It can model the beginning of the universe, but it cannot explain why there is something rather than nothing.

These questions belong to philosophy, theology, and metaphysics—disciplines that scientism dismisses, yet cannot replace.

The Need for a Broader Framework

In earlier chapters, we saw that logic, mathematics, and moral law are immaterial realities. Science depends on these, yet they are not products of science. They are part of a broader framework of truth that points beyond the physical world.

By insisting that only the measurable is real, scientism blinds itself to the very foundations science rests upon.

The Human Cost of Scientism

When scientism rules, anything that cannot be measured is dismissed as irrelevant. Human dignity becomes a biological construct. Purpose becomes an illusion. Spiritual life is seen as a delusion. This reductionism strips life of meaning and people of value.

History shows the danger: when humans are seen only as physical objects, they can be treated as disposable resources. The atrocities of the twentieth century were often justified with pseudo-scientific language.

Science in Its Proper Place

Science flourishes when it operates within its proper bounds—studying the natural world while recognizing that there is more to reality than the natural world. The greatest scientists in history, from Newton to Einstein, saw their work as uncovering the mind of God, not replacing him.

Bridge to the Next Chapter

Scientism seeks to replace God with a microscope. Atheistic humanism seeks to replace him with ourselves. In the next chapter, we will see why humanity cannot bear the weight of being its own god.

Chapter 5

Atheistic Humanism
The Impossible Task of Being Our Own God

ATHEISTIC HUMANISM IS THE belief that humanity can define its own purpose, morality, and destiny without God. It celebrates human reason, creativity, and autonomy—but removes the Creator from the picture. In doing so, it places on humanity a burden it cannot bear.

The Rise of Atheistic Humanism

Emerging strongly during the Enlightenment, atheistic humanism sought to free humanity from what it saw as the oppressive weight of religion. It promised a future built on reason, equality, and progress—a golden age where humanity would guide itself. But history has shown that when humanity makes itself the highest authority, it inevitably repeats the sins it sought to escape.

The Weight of Moral Authority

Without God, humanism must invent its own moral code. But morality without a higher authority is fragile—subject to change with culture, politics, and personal preference. What one generation celebrates, the next can condemn. The result is moral instability, where nothing is truly fixed.

Earlier in this book, we saw how relativism and materialism erode truth and meaning. Atheistic humanism inherits both flaws. It tries to keep the moral vision of the gospel without the God of the gospel, ignoring that the vision depends on the God it rejects.

The Burden of Ultimate Purpose

To be your own god means carrying the weight of defining why you exist. But humans are finite, limited in knowledge, and bound by mortality. We cannot create ultimate meaning for ourselves any more than we can create the universe itself. Without God, purpose becomes a temporary illusion, vanishing at death.

The Illusion of Progress

Atheistic humanism often claims that humanity is evolving morally—that education, technology, and enlightened thinking will make us better.

Yet, the twentieth century, with its world wars and genocides, was the bloodiest in history. Progress without God is progress without a compass.

The God We Cannot Replace

The irony is that atheistic humanism depends on values—human dignity, justice, equality—that flow from the biblical worldview. Remove God and these values lose their foundation. You can affirm them as preferences but not as universal truths.

Bridge to the Next Chapter

Atheistic humanism tries to enthrone humanity; postmodernism tries to dismantle even the idea of a central truth. In the next chapter, we will see how postmodernism's rejection of grand narratives leads to the fragmentation of meaning itself.

Chapter 6

Postmodernism
The Death of Meaning

POSTMODERNISM IS A CULTURAL and philosophical movement that rejects the idea of universal truth. It arose in the late twentieth century as a reaction to modernism's confidence in reason, science, and progress. If modernism said, "We can discover the truth," postmodernism says, "There is no truth to discover—only perspectives."

The Rejection of Grand Narratives

Postmodernism denies what it calls "grand narratives"—overarching stories that claim to explain reality. The biblical account of creation, fall, and redemption is such a narrative. So is the Enlightenment vision of reason leading to progress. In the postmodern view, all such narratives are tools of power, used to control others.

The Fragmentation of Reality

If there is no overarching truth, then reality is reduced to isolated experiences. Each person has their own truth, their own meaning, their own reality. This radical subjectivity sounds liberating, but it leaves individuals disconnected, adrift in a sea of personal interpretations.

In earlier chapters, we saw how relativism erodes truth. Postmodernism takes this further—it denies that truth even exists.

The Cultural Consequences

When truth dies, meaning dies with it. Without a shared understanding of reality, societies fracture into tribes, each with its own narrative and language. Dialogue becomes impossible because there is no agreement on the basic terms of discussion.

This is why debates over morality, identity, and even biology can feel so hopeless today. Postmodernism removes the foundation for resolving such questions.

The Spiritual Cost

Postmodernism offers no hope beyond personal preference. It leaves people searching for meaning in temporary pleasures, political movements, or self-expression—none of which can bear the weight of the human soul.

The gospel offers something postmodernism cannot: a truth that is both universal and personal, a narrative that is both cosmic and intimate. It tells us who we are, where we came from, and where we are going—not as an instrument of control but as the revelation of a loving Creator.

Bridge to the Next Chapter

If postmodernism denies truth and meaning, the next worldview we will examine seeks to replace them with an ancient lie in a modern disguise: the revival of paganism and pantheism in contemporary spirituality.

Chapter 7

Paganism and Pantheism
The Old Gods in New Disguise

While modern secular culture often claims to have moved beyond religion, a surprising number of its spiritual trends are not new at all. They are revivals of ancient pagan and pantheistic beliefs—the worship of nature, the deification of the self, and the blending of all gods into one.

The Return of the Old Gods

Paganism never truly disappeared. It was pushed to the margins by the spread of Christianity, but its core ideas have resurfaced in movements like neo-paganism, Wicca, and certain strands of the New Age. These systems often romanticize ancient nature worship and celebrate polytheism as more "inclusive" than monotheism.

Pantheism in Modern Disguise

Pantheism—the belief that God is everything and everything is God—has become especially popular through environmental spirituality, Eastern mysticism, and self-help philosophies. It denies the distinction between Creator and creation, reducing God to an impersonal energy or universal consciousness.

This may sound harmless or even uplifting, but it erases God's moral authority. If God is everything, then God is also cruelty, injustice, and evil. There is no moral line to cross because all is equally "divine."

The Appeal of Paganism and Pantheism

In a fragmented, postmodern world, these beliefs offer a sense of connection—to nature, to each other, to the universe. They avoid the "offense" of exclusive truth claims and promise a spirituality without judgment. But in doing so, they strip God of his holiness and justice, replacing him with a projection of our own desires.

The Biblical Response

Scripture is clear: creation is not God, but it reveals God (Rom 1:20).

Worshiping creation instead of the Creator is the oldest form of idolatry. The Bible presents God as both utterly transcendent (above all creation) and deeply personal (present with his people).

This balance—God's greatness and God's intimacy—is lost in pagan and pantheistic systems. They offer connection without accountability, wonder without worship, and spirituality without truth.

Bridge to the Next Chapter

As we turn to the next chapter, we will see how one of the most persistent falsehoods—the idea that all religions are essentially the same—combines elements of relativism, paganism, and postmodernism into a single, seductive lie.

Chapter 8

All Religions Are the Same
The Seductive Lie of Spiritual Equality

Few ideas feel as polite, progressive, and peaceful as the statement, "All religions are basically the same." It's a belief that allows a person to nod in agreement with everyone, to avoid conflict, and to appear open-minded. It sounds like tolerance, but it is built on a foundation of half-truths and, ultimately, deception.

The Modern Origin of the Lie

The idea that all religions are equal in truth and value is not ancient wisdom. It is largely a modern development, rooted in the Enlightenment's emphasis on human reason, nineteenth-century romanticism, and the twentieth-century desire for global peace after two devastating world wars. Philosophers and political leaders began to argue that religion itself was a cause of conflict, and therefore, the solution was to flatten out the differences—to see every faith as simply one cultural expression of a universal spiritual reality.

This thinking gained momentum in interfaith movements, the popularization of Eastern philosophies in the West, and the rise of pluralistic democracies where no single faith was privileged.

The United Nations' language of mutual respect between all religions further cemented this in the cultural imagination.[1]

Why the Idea Is Seductive

This belief appeals to our longing for unity. It allows people of different faiths to sit in the same room, smile at one another, and feel they have transcended division. It avoids the awkwardness of telling someone they might be wrong. It also relieves a person from having to seriously investigate their own faith—if all paths are equal, then spiritual laziness is not a danger.

But there is a fatal flaw: if truth matters, then contradictions cannot be swept away with a slogan.

The Irreconcilable Differences

Let's test the claim. Christianity teaches that Jesus is the eternal Son of God, who became human, died for our sins, and rose again—and that salvation comes only through him. Islam denies his divinity, denies his crucifixion, and teaches salvation through submission to Allah's law. Hinduism embraces many gods and views salvation as liberation from the cycle of rebirth through various possible paths. Buddhism teaches that there is no personal God at all, only the extinguishing of desire in order to achieve enlightenment.

These are not small differences in ritual or terminology—they are direct contradictions about who God is, what humanity's problem is, and how that problem is solved. If all are "equally true," then truth itself has no meaning.

The Logical Collapse

If two statements contradict each other, they cannot both be true in the same sense at the same time. This is not narrow-minded dogma; it is basic logic. To say "Jesus is God" and "Jesus is not

---

1. United Nations, "Declaration."

God" are both true is to abandon reason itself. And if reason is abandoned, then no claim—including the claim that all religions are the same—has any weight.

The Biblical Position

Far from endorsing religious pluralism, Scripture consistently warns against it. In Isa 45:5, God says, "I am the Lord, and there is no other; apart from me there is no God." Jesus himself declared in John 14:6, "I am the way and the truth and the life. No one comes to the Father except through me." These statements are not compatible with the idea that all religions are equally valid.

The Moral Consequence of the Lie

If all religions are the same, then moral differences vanish, too. Faiths that promote peace are placed on the same level as faiths that justify violence. Systems that protect human dignity are equated with those that degrade it. Such false equality rewards the harmful and undermines the good.

A True Basis for Unity

True unity is not built on pretending that contradictions do not exist. It is built on truth, justice, and love—all of which find their fullest expression in the gospel. In Christ, unity is not an erasure of differences but a reconciliation of people to God and to each other on the basis of truth.

Closing Reflection

The claim that all religions are the same may sound humble, but it is actually an act of arrogance—deciding that the deepest convictions of billions can be redefined with a single sweeping statement.

True humility is to listen to what each faith truly teaches, examine the evidence, and follow the truth wherever it leads.

If the gospel is true—and the historical, moral, and spiritual evidence points to the fact that it is—then it is not loving to hide it in the name of politeness. The most compassionate act is to invite others to discover what no other faith can offer: the grace of God in Christ, given freely to all who believe.

Chapter 9

The Problem of Evil

How Other Worldviews Avoid the Hardest Question

FEW QUESTIONS STRIKE THE human heart more deeply than this: If God is good and all-powerful, why does evil exist? The problem of evil has been called the greatest challenge to faith. But it is also the greatest challenge to every worldview, not just Christianity.

The Universal Dilemma

Every worldview—whether religious, philosophical, or secular—must answer why suffering and injustice exist. For the atheist, pain is simply an unfortunate byproduct of a mindless universe. For some Eastern philosophies, evil is an illusion to be transcended.[1] For certain forms of paganism, evil is necessary for cosmic balance.[2] These answers might dull the edge of the question for some, but they do not satisfy the cry for justice that is written into the human soul.

---

1. Śaṅkara, Brahma Sūtra Bhāṣya, I.1.1; Rahula, *What the Buddha Taught*.
2. Dalley, *Myths from Mesopotamia*; Burkert, *Ancient Mystery Cults*.

The Cry for Justice

When a child suffers, when an innocent is murdered, when corruption crushes the poor, we do not simply observe events; we recoil in moral outrage. This outrage is evidence that we expect the world to be different from what it is. But if there is no ultimate standard of good and evil, then such outrage is only a survival instinct, a quirk of evolution. It loses its moral weight.

And yet, even those who deny objective morality live as if some acts are truly wrong and others truly right. This is the contradiction: to feel the force of evil but to deny the framework that makes it truly evil.

The Inadequacy of Other Explanations

- *Atheism/Naturalism*—If everything is the result of blind chance, then "evil" is just a human label for what we dislike. There is no cosmic injustice, only events.

- *Eastern Mysticism*—If suffering is an illusion, then compassion itself becomes unnecessary—and the deepest human instincts to help the suffering are reduced to mistakes of perception.

- *Relativism*—If morality is relative, then the word "evil" becomes meaningless, and no one can condemn anything—including genocide, slavery, or abuse—without imposing personal preference as law.

- *Pagan Dualism*—If good and evil are equal and eternal forces, then there is no hope for ultimate victory, only an endless struggle.

Each of these systems, when pressed, either denies the reality of evil, diminishes it, or makes peace with its permanence.

Why the Question Persists

The problem of evil does not go away because we know, deep down, that evil is not simply "the way things are." We know it is an intruder. It is parasitic—feeding on what is good but never able to create anything itself. Our longing for justice is evidence that we were made for a reality where justice is fulfilled.

The Opening for the Gospel

When people dismiss Christianity because of the problem of evil, they often fail to see that Christianity does not run from the question. It stares it in the face. The Bible contains accounts of genocide, betrayal, plague, famine, and personal agony. Its writers lament openly and protest to God himself. This honesty is rare in religious literature.

The gospel's strength is not that it sidesteps the question but that it provides a context in which suffering and evil are confronted, judged, and ultimately defeated.

Closing Reflection

Every worldview must give an account of why evil exists and what will be done about it. Most offer resignation, denial, or endless cycles. Christianity offers something else entirely—not just an explanation but a resolution. And that resolution begins with a God who takes the problem of evil so seriously that he enters the story himself.

Chapter 10

The Christian Answer to Suffering and Evil

THE PROBLEM OF EVIL is not answered by clever philosophy alone—it demands an answer from reality itself. Christianity dares to offer one, not by avoiding the question but by stepping directly into its center.

It is an answer unlike any other: God himself enters the world of suffering.

God Does Not Watch from Afar

In most religious systems, the divine remains distant, untouched by pain. The gods of mythology live in comfort while mortals suffer below. Even in many philosophical views of God, He is seen as an impersonal force—too exalted or too detached to bleed.

The gospel tells a different story. Jesus Christ, the eternal Word through whom all things were made, took on flesh and walked among us. He did not simply witness suffering; he tasted it. He was betrayed, beaten, mocked, and nailed to a cross. The Creator of life experienced the full weight of death.

The Cross as the Center of the Answer

The cross is not an abstract theological symbol—it is God's personal engagement with evil. On that hill outside Jerusalem, God absorbed into himself the very worst the world could offer: hatred, violence, injustice, abandonment. And he did it willingly.

By dying, Jesus exposed the true nature of evil—that it destroys, corrupts, and kills. By rising, he demonstrated its defeat. The resurrection is not just proof of life after death; it is proof that evil cannot have the final word.

Suffering Transformed

Christianity does not promise a life free of suffering; it promises that suffering will not be wasted. Romans 8:28 declares that "in all things God works for the good of those who love him." This is not a cheap platitude. It is a radical claim that even tragedy can be woven into a greater story of redemption.

Countless testimonies bear this out: addicts freed, enemies reconciled, grieving parents comforted in ways that defy explanation. These are not denials of pain—they are transformations of it.

The Hope That Anchors

The Christian hope is not in avoiding the valley but in knowing that the valley has an end. Revelation 21:4 promises that God "will wipe every tear from their eyes. There will be no more death or mourning or crying or pain, for the old order of things has passed away."

This is not symbolic poetry—it is the destination toward which all of history is moving. Evil is not eternal. It has an expiration date.

The Uniqueness of the Christian Answer

No other worldview offers this combination:

The Christian Answer to Suffering and Evil

- a God who is both all-powerful and deeply personal
- a clear moral diagnosis of evil
- a concrete historical event (the cross and resurrection) as the turning point in the battle
- a promised future where justice and mercy meet perfectly

Closing Reflection

The Christian answer to suffering does not explain away every mystery, nor does it pretend that pain is easy to endure. What it does is offer an unshakable foundation: the God who made you has entered your suffering, carried your sin, and guaranteed that evil's days are numbered.

In a world desperate for hope, the cross and the empty tomb stand as God's unchanging testimony: "I have seen your tears. I have heard your cries. And I am making all things new."

Chapter 11

The Uniqueness of the Gospel in a World of Competing Truths

We live in a world overflowing with truth claims. Every culture, every religion, every philosophy offers its own explanation of life's origin, meaning, morality, and destiny. The marketplace of ideas is not new, but it has never been more global, more accessible, and more insistent than it is today.

In this environment, the gospel of Jesus Christ stands not as one option among many but as the singular truth that fulfills humanity's deepest needs and answers life's hardest questions.

A Faith Rooted in History

Many spiritual systems are built on the private visions of a single individual, unverifiable by history. The gospel is different. It is grounded in events that occurred in a specific place and time, witnessed by many, and recorded in detail. The life, death, and resurrection of Jesus of Nazareth are not mythological archetypes; they are historical realities.

The Uniqueness of the Gospel in a World of Competing Truths

Even skeptical historians acknowledge that Jesus lived, that he was crucified under Pontius Pilate,[1] and that his followers believed they encountered him alive afterward.[2] The question is not whether these events happened but how to explain them.

A Diagnosis the World Cannot Imitate

The gospel's understanding of the human condition is unparalleled. It does not flatter us by saying we are basically good people who need a little improvement. It tells the uncomfortable truth: we are rebels at heart, separated from God by sin, unable to save ourselves.

Other systems offer advice, disciplines, or laws to follow in the hope of improvement. The gospel offers something no other faith dares: the Creator himself bearing the cost of our rebellion so we can be forgiven and restored.

Grace Without Rival

Every other religion, in its own way, sets a ladder for humanity to climb toward the divine. The rungs may be rituals, moral laws, meditation, or enlightenment, but the burden is on us to ascend.

The gospel reverses the direction. God descends to us. He takes the initiative, accomplishes the rescue, and offers it freely as a gift. This is grace—unearned, undeserved, and unrepayable.

Truth That Transforms

Truth is not simply information to be agreed with; it is reality to be lived in. The gospel not only forgives but transforms, producing in believers a love, humility, and courage that cannot be manufactured by willpower alone.

---

1. Ehrman, *Did Jesus Exist?*; Lüdemann, *Resurrection of Christ*.
2. Fredriksen, *Jesus of Nazareth*; Sanders, *Historical Figure of Jesus*.

From the first-century church that turned the Roman Empire upside down without armies or wealth, to modern believers who risk their lives to share Christ, the transformative power of the gospel is unchanged.

The Futility of Counterfeits

Many worldviews borrow fragments of gospel truth—compassion, justice, human dignity—but they lack the foundation to sustain them. Cut off from the source, these borrowed virtues eventually decay into mere preferences, vulnerable to redefinition.

Without the gospel, even the noblest ideals drift. With it, they find their true anchor.

Closing Reflection

In a noisy world of competing truths, the gospel's uniqueness is not arrogance—it is reality. It is the only message in which God's justice and mercy meet perfectly, in which death is defeated, and in which love is not a human aspiration but a divine gift.

The choice before every person is not between "religion" and "no religion" but between truth and illusion. The gospel does not beg for a place at the table of ideas; it invites the world to a feast prepared by the King himself.

PART 4

Standing Firm
Living the Truth in an Age of Deception

Chapter 1

The Age of Deception

WE LIVE IN AN age where deception is not only common but celebrated. Lies are packaged as compassion, half-truths are sold as wisdom, and moral compromise is disguised as progress. Technology has made information instant and limitless, but it has also blurred the lines between truth and falsehood until many no longer know what to believe.

The Bible warned us of such days. Jesus himself said, "Watch out that no one deceives you. For many will come in my name, claiming, 'I am the Messiah,' and will deceive many" (Matt 24:4–5). The apostle Paul wrote of a time when people would "gather around them a great number of teachers to say what their itching ears want to hear" (2 Tim 4:3). That time is not coming—it is here.

The Subtle Nature of Modern Lies

The most dangerous lies are rarely outright fabrications; they are truths twisted just enough to mislead.

Modern deception often cloaks itself in moral language—"love," "justice," "equality"—but redefines these terms according to cultural trends rather than God's standard. In doing so, it empties them of their true power.

Consider how the biblical command to love has been reinterpreted to mean "never judge," ignoring that real love sometimes confronts for the sake of truth, or how the pursuit of justice has been severed from the concept of righteousness, producing movements that rage against certain evils while embracing others.

Historical Parallels

This is not the first time truth has been under assault. The Roman Empire demanded loyalty to Caesar above all else, branding early Christians as traitors because they confessed, "Jesus is Lord." In the Middle Ages, corrupt leaders distorted the gospel to maintain power. In every generation, the faithful have had to choose between comfort and conviction.

The difference today is speed and scale. Deception can now circle the globe in seconds, shaping millions of minds before truth has a chance to respond.

Why Deception Works

Deception works because it appeals to our desires. Eve was not tricked into eating the forbidden fruit by a monstrous figure with obvious malice; she was persuaded that it was "good for food and pleasing to the eye, and also desirable for gaining wisdom" (Gen 3:6). Lies still work the same way—they present something good but in the wrong way, at the wrong time, or apart from God.

Modern culture tells us we can define our own truth, shape our own identity, and determine our own morality. It flatters human pride while removing any accountability to the Creator. This is why deception is so seductive: it promises freedom while delivering slavery.

Standing Firm in a Shifting World

To resist deception, we must first love the truth. This means more than knowing Bible verses—it means submitting our thoughts, desires, and actions to God's word even when it contradicts our preferences. Truth is not something we shape; it is something that shapes us.

- *Know the Word*—The more familiar we are with Scripture, the easier it is to spot counterfeits.
- *Test the Spirits*—As 1 John 4:1 says, "do not believe every spirit, but test the spirits to see whether they are from God."
- *Stay in Community*—Lone believers are easier to deceive. A community grounded in truth offers accountability and clarity.
- *Pray for Discernment*—Wisdom is not gained by intellect alone. It is a gift from God for those who ask.

Closing Reflection

We are not called to survive this age of deception by hiding in fear but to shine as lights in the darkness. This requires courage—the courage to speak truth when it's unpopular, to live with integrity when compromise is rewarded, and to hold fast to Christ when the world offers easier paths.

The age of deception is also the age of opportunity. Every lie exposed is a chance to point someone to the One who is "the way, the truth, and the life" (John 14:6). In a world drowning in confusion, the believer who stands firm becomes a lighthouse—not because of their own brilliance but because they reflect the unchanging light of Christ.

Chapter 2

Courage in the Face of the Crowd

IT IS EASY TO follow the truth when it costs nothing. It is far harder when the cost is your comfort, your reputation, or your safety. Yet every generation of believers has faced the moment when standing for God meant standing alone. We live in a time when the crowd is louder than ever. Social media amplifies popular opinion, news cycles reward outrage, and public figures rise or fall on the shifting winds of cultural approval. To stand for biblical truth in such an environment often feels like standing against an ocean tide—and yet, that is exactly what we are called to do.

The Danger of the Crowd

The Bible is filled with warnings about the crowd. It was the crowd that shouted "Crucify him!" on the day Jesus stood trial. It was the crowd that demanded Aaron make a golden calf when Moses was on the mountain. Crowds can be swayed by emotion, fear, and self-interest far more quickly than they can be persuaded by truth.

Modern culture prizes inclusion and consensus, often at the expense of conviction. We are told that to disagree is to divide, and to divide is the ultimate sin. But true unity is not found in the absence of conflict; it is found in shared commitment to what is right.

Biblical Examples of Standing Alone

Consider Daniel, who refused to defile himself with the king's food even when every other young exile probably did. Or Elijah, who stood on Mount Carmel against hundreds of prophets of Baal. Or Esther, who risked her life to approach the king and plead for her people. In each case, courage was not the absence of fear but the decision to act in spite of it.

Even Paul, abandoned by many of his companions, wrote in 2 Tim 4:16–17, "At my first defense, no one came to my support, but everyone deserted me. But the Lord stood at my side and gave me strength."

Why Courage Matters Now More Than Ever

In an age of deception, courage is not optional. Lies gain power when truth is silenced, and truth is often silenced because people fear the cost of speaking it. But silence in the face of falsehood is not neutrality; it is consent.

When believers lack courage, society drifts toward moral chaos. When they find their voice, even a small minority can change the course of history. The Reformation began with a single monk nailing his convictions to a church door. The abolition of the slave trade was advanced by a handful of men and women who refused to accept the status quo.

How to Stand Courageously

- *Anchor Yourself in God's Word*—Courage built on opinion will crumble. Courage built on God's truth stands firm.

- *Accept the Cost*—Jesus warned that following him would mean taking up our cross. We should expect opposition, not be surprised by it.
- *Seek God's Approval Over Man's*—The fear of man leads to compromise; the fear of God leads to faithfulness.
- *Remember You Are Not Alone*—Even if no human stands with you, Christ himself is at your side.

Closing Reflection

The crowd will always find reasons to justify compromise. They will say, "Just this once," or "It's not a big deal," or "Everyone else is doing it." But courage listens to a different voice—the still, small voice of the Spirit that whispers, "This is the way; walk in it" (Isa 30:21).

History does not remember those who blended into the crowd. It remembers those who, at the critical moment, stood apart. The courage to face the crowd is not arrogance or stubbornness; it is loyalty to the One who stood for us when we could not stand for ourselves.

Chapter 3

The War for Reality
Truth Under Siege

Every generation faces its battles, but ours is unique: we are fighting for reality itself. In previous centuries, wars were fought over territory, kingship, or resources. Today's war is fought over truth—not just what is right and wrong but what is real and unreal. The stakes could not be higher, because when truth becomes subjective, reality becomes negotiable and morality collapses.

The Subtle Redefinition of Truth

Modern culture has shifted from believing in truth as an objective reality to treating it as a personal possession. We hear phrases like "my truth" and "your truth," as though reality bends to fit our preferences. This is not simply linguistic laziness—it is a deliberate reprogramming of how people think. The Bible warns of this drift. Isaiah 5:20 says, "Woe to those who call evil good and good evil, who put darkness for light and light for darkness." Once society detaches truth from God, it becomes vulnerable to any narrative powerful enough to sway the crowd.

The Tools of the Siege

- *Relativism*—The belief that all truths are equally valid. In practice, it erases the concept of falsehood altogether.

- *Misinformation*—Not just accidental error, but the strategic flooding of lies so that truth is drowned out in noise.

- *Emotional Manipulation*—Truth is replaced by what feels right in the moment, creating a moral compass that spins wildly with each new cultural fad.

- *Language Corruption*—Words are redefined to fit political or ideological goals, shifting public perception without changing facts. History has seen this before. Totalitarian regimes of the twentieth century understood that controlling language was the first step to controlling thought. What is alarming today is that this is happening globally, not just within single nations.

The Christian Response

We are not the first to live in an age when truth was under siege. The early church proclaimed Christ as Lord in a Roman Empire that declared Caesar to be god. Reformers like Martin Luther stood against the institutional distortions of their day. In each case, victory began not with armies but with individuals who refused to yield to the lies around them. Our calling is the same today:

- *Anchor to Scripture*—God's word is the unchanging reference point in a shifting culture.

- *Discern the Times*—Recognize the tactics used to distort truth so we are not deceived.

- *Speak Boldly*—Silence is the oxygen of deception; truth must be spoken, even when costly.

- *Live Consistently*—Hypocrisy destroys credibility faster than persecution can.

The Cost of Inaction

When truth is abandoned, the void is filled by the loudest voices and the most aggressive agendas. History shows that lies, once normalized, lead to oppression, injustice, and destruction. If Christians retreat from the battle for truth, we abandon not only the culture but also the generations to come.

Closing Reflection

Jesus said in John 8:32, "Then you will know the truth, and the truth will set you free." But freedom is not automatic; it must be guarded. In an age where deception is celebrated, defending truth is an act of war—a war worth fighting, because without truth, love loses its anchor, justice loses its meaning, and faith loses its foundation. The war for reality is here. We must not lose it.

Chapter 4

When Silence Becomes Complicity

SILENCE HAS ALWAYS BEEN a choice, but in an age of deception, it becomes a weapon—not in the hands of the righteous but in the arsenal of the liar. When truth is attacked and we remain silent, we allow falsehood to advance unchecked. History shows us that the great evils of the past did not require the majority to commit atrocities; they only required the majority to say nothing.

The Illusion of Neutrality

Many believe that by staying out of cultural and moral debates, they are taking a neutral stance. But neutrality in the face of evil is an illusion. Jesus said in Matt 12:30, "Whoever is not with me is against me." There is no spiritual Switzerland. When the early church was pressured to keep quiet about the resurrection, Peter and John replied in Acts 4:20, "As for us, we cannot help speaking about what we have seen and heard." To be silent would have been to deny the truth they knew firsthand.

The High Cost of Speaking

Speaking up for God's truth often comes with a price—social rejection, professional loss, even persecution. Yet the price of silence is always higher. It erodes our integrity, compromises our witness, and allows darkness to fill the void where light should shine. The Hebrew prophets understood this. Jeremiah spoke God's words in a time when false prophets promised peace, and for his honesty, he was beaten and thrown into a cistern. Still, he declared, "His word is in my heart like a fire, a fire shut up in my bones. I am weary of holding it in; indeed, I cannot."

Cultural Pressure and Self-Censorship

Today, the cost of truth is amplified by social media outrage, cancel culture, and ideological gatekeeping. These forces thrive on intimidation, seeking to make examples of anyone who defies the prevailing narrative. The result is self-censorship—a slow retreat from honesty until the truth is spoken only in whispers, if at all. But when believers yield to this pressure, the enemy's work becomes easier, not harder.

Why Speaking Matters

- *Silence Protects Lies*—Without opposition, deception gains the appearance of legitimacy.
- *Truth Builds Courage*—Each act of speaking truth emboldens others to do the same.
- *Faith Requires Confession*—Romans 10:9 links salvation with openly declaring that Jesus is Lord.
- *Generations Are Watching*—Our children and communities learn not from what we say we believe but from whether we live it out publicly.

The Courage to Break the Silence

Breaking silence does not always require a public platform; it begins in our everyday conversations. It means refusing to laugh at the joke that mocks God, gently challenging the statement that denies his truth, and offering hope where despair has settled. Courage grows in small acts before it is tested in great ones.

Closing Reflection

When we stand before God, we will not be asked whether we managed to stay out of trouble with the world, but whether we were faithful to him. In an age where deception thrives on quiet compliance, speaking the truth is not merely an option—it is an obligation. The time to speak is always now because the longer we wait, the louder the lie becomes.

Chapter 5

The Courage to Stand Alone

STANDING ALONE IS NEVER comfortable. We are wired for community, drawn to the safety of agreement, and encouraged by the strength of numbers. Yet the history of God's people is full of moments when the majority was wrong, and the faithful were forced to stand apart. In such moments, courage is not found in crowds but in conviction.

The Loneliness of Conviction

Noah built the ark while the world mocked him. Daniel prayed openly when it was illegal. The prophets often spoke to audiences who despised their message. Each faced the same inner battle: the ache of isolation and the temptation to blend in. What set them apart was their willingness to obey God rather than seek human approval.

The Source of True Courage

Courage to stand alone does not come from self-confidence but from God-confidence. David's boldness before Goliath was rooted in his trust in the Lord's deliverance. Paul's endurance through imprisonment and persecution came from the assurance that he was serving a higher King. When we believe God's truth more than we fear man's rejection, we find the strength to stand.

Recognizing the Cost

Standing alone may cost relationships, opportunities, or even personal safety. Jesus warned his disciples that following him would bring division, even within families. But he also promised that those who endure to the end will be saved. This eternal perspective reframes the sacrifice—temporary loss for everlasting gain.

Practical Steps to Stand Alone

- *Anchor Your Identity in Christ*—If your worth is tied to others' approval, you will compromise to keep it.
- *Prepare Before the Test*—Resolve your convictions in advance so you are not swayed in the moment.
- *Seek Strength in Prayer*—Solitude with God strengthens you for solitude before men.
- *Remember the Witnesses*—Hebrews 12 speaks of a great cloud of witnesses who cheer us on in the race of faith.

Encouragement for the Isolated

When you stand alone for God, you are never truly alone. Elijah felt abandoned until God revealed that thousands in Israel had not bowed to Baal. Even if you see no allies, heaven's hosts surround you, and God himself stands with you.

Closing Reflection

The courage to stand alone is not about defiance for its own sake; it is about loyalty to the One who stood alone for us on the cross. In a world that drifts with the current, the solitary figure who stands for truth becomes a lighthouse—a fixed point by which others can find their way. When you stand with God, you stand on the side that will, in the end, be the only one still standing.

Chapter 6

Faith Under Fire
Standing True in Trials

FAITH IS MOST CONVINCING when it is tested. Words spoken in comfort hold little weight until they are proven in the heat of trial. The Scriptures are filled with accounts of men and women whose belief in God was forged in fire—not metaphorical fire alone but sometimes literal flames.

Why Trials Come

Trials are not random accidents in the believer's life. They are allowed by God for a purpose—to refine, to reveal, and to ready us for greater service. James 1:2–3 tells us to "consider it pure joy" when we face trials because the testing of our faith produces perseverance. Perseverance is not born in ease but in endurance.

Biblical Portraits of Faith Under Fire

Shadrach, Meshach, and Abednego refused to bow to the golden image, even under threat of a furnace. Their declaration, "The God we serve is able to deliver us . . . but even if he does not, we will not serve your gods," remains one of the clearest pictures of unshakable faith.[1] Daniel faced the lions' den with similar resolve, choosing prayer to God over obedience to men.[2] In the New Testament, Paul endured beatings, shipwrecks, and imprisonment, yet declared, "I know whom I have believed."[3]

The Nature of Tested Faith

Faith that has never been challenged can be shallow, built on borrowed convictions or untested assumptions. But faith that survives hardship gains depth and power. It becomes a testimony—not of our strength but of God's sustaining grace.

How to Stand True in Trials

- *Remember God's Past Faithfulness*—Recalling his previous deliverance fuels present courage.
- *Keep Your Eyes on the Eternal*—Trials are temporary; the reward is everlasting.
- *Surround Yourself with the Faithful*—Even the strongest believer can falter in isolation.
- *Pray Without Ceasing*—Communion with God keeps your spirit anchored when the storm rages.

The Witness of Endurance

The world is watching how Christians respond to suffering. When we endure with peace, hope, and unwavering trust, we preach the gospel without words. Our trials become a pulpit, our perseverance a sermon, and our deliverance—or even our steadfastness unto death—a declaration that Christ is worth more than life itself.

1. Dan 3:16–18.
2. Dan 6:10.
3. 2 Tim 1:12.

Closing Reflection

Faith under fire strips away pretense and exposes what we truly believe. It is in the flames of trial that the gold of our trust is refined, and the dross of doubt is burned away. When the heat comes—and it will—let it be said of us that we stood firm, not because we were fearless but because we trusted the One who walks with us in the fire.

Chapter 7

The Cost of Compromise

COMPROMISE IS RARELY SUDDEN. It begins subtly—a small concession here, a quiet avoidance there—until what was once unthinkable becomes normal. In the life of faith, compromise corrodes conviction and gradually aligns the believer with the world's values rather than God's truth.

The First Step Away

The first compromise often seems harmless. A word left unsaid to avoid offense. A truth softened to gain approval. But every step away from full obedience makes the next step easier. Lot's choice to settle near Sodom eventually led to his family's moral and spiritual collapse. Samson's repeated compromises with Delilah dulled his discernment until he could no longer see the danger before him.

Why Compromise Is So Dangerous

- *It Redefines Truth*—Small distortions accumulate until the standard of God's word is replaced by cultural norms.
- *It Weakens Witness*—The world sees when believers live inconsistently, and it undermines the credibility of the gospel.

- *It Invites Greater Temptation*—Each compromise lowers resistance to the next, creating a downward spiral.
- *It Offends God*—Revelation 3 warns against lukewarm faith, which provokes God's rejection more than outright opposition.

The Allure of Acceptance

Many compromises are driven by the desire to belong. We fear being labeled intolerant, divisive, or extreme. But Jesus warned that the world would hate his followers because it hated him first. The approval of men may feel comforting in the moment, but it comes at the cost of divine favor.

Guarding Against Compromise

- *Know the Word*—A strong grasp of Scripture allows you to recognize when a choice conflicts with God's commands.
- *Set Boundaries*—Decide in advance which lines you will never cross, no matter the pressure.
- *Stay Accountable*—Trusted believers can help you see blind spots and stand firm.
- *Live with Eternity in View*—The praise of men fades quickly; the reward of God endures forever.

Examples of Uncompromising Faith

Daniel refused the king's food that violated God's law, even though it risked his position.[1] The apostles chose to obey God rather than men, fully aware it could cost their lives. Such examples remind us that compromise may be common, but it is not inevitable.

---

1. Dan 1:8.

Closing Reflection

Every believer must choose daily between the narrow path of obedience and the wide road of compromise. The cost of standing firm is real, but the cost of surrendering ground is far greater. When faced with the temptation to yield, remember that Christ never compromised in his mission to save us. We honor him best by holding to the truth without dilution, no matter the price.

Chapter 8

Strength in the Secret Place

Public strength is born in private surrender. The believer who stands firm before men is the one who has first bowed low before God. The "secret place"—a life of prayer, meditation, and quiet fellowship with the Lord—is where convictions are forged, hearts are steadied, and faith is renewed.

The Biblical Pattern

Before facing Goliath, David spent years alone with God in the fields, learning to trust him in danger and obscurity.[1] Before beginning his public ministry, Jesus withdrew into the wilderness for forty days of fasting and prayer.[2] Before the cross, he sought strength in Gethsemane, wrestling with the Father in the stillness of night.[3] Again and again, Scripture shows that great public victories are prepared in hidden places.

1. 1 Sam 16:11–13, 17:34–37.
2. Matt 4:1; Luke 4:1–2; Matt 26:36–44.
3. Luke 22:39–46.

Why the Secret Place Matters

- *It Anchors Your Identity*—In the secret place, you are known not for your work, your role, or your reputation but as a child of God.
- *It Refines Your Perspective*—Away from the noise, you see the world and your trials in the light of eternity.
- *It Strengthens Your Resolve*—Time with God equips you to face pressures without compromise.
- *It Deepens Intimacy*—Faith is not a set of principles to defend but a relationship to nurture.

The Battle for the Secret Place

The enemy knows the power of a believer rooted in God's presence. That is why distraction, busyness, and endless noise are some of his most effective weapons. Neglecting the secret place weakens your defenses long before you face a public test.

How to Cultivate the Secret Place

- *Set a Time*—Guard it as you would any important appointment.
- *Choose a Place*—A consistent space helps train your heart and mind to focus.
- *Be Still*—Silence before God is often where his voice is clearest.
- *Pray Honestly*—Pour out your heart without pretension; he knows it already.
- *Listen*—Let Scripture and the Spirit speak to you before you speak to others.

The Overflow Effect

Those who dwell in the secret place carry its fragrance into the world. Moses descended from the mountain with a face that shone from God's glory.[4] Peter and John, though uneducated, spoke with such boldness that the rulers "recognized that they had been with Jesus."[5] The secret place is not an escape from the world but preparation to enter it with the power of God.

Closing Reflection

Strength in the secret place is not optional for those who want to stand in the evil day—it is essential. The world will not see those hours alone with God, but they will see the unshakable peace, the quiet courage, and the steadfast love that flow from them. In a noisy, distracted age, the most radical act may simply be to close the door, kneel before the Father, and emerge carrying the strength of his presence.

---

4. Exod 34:29-35.
5. Acts 4:13.

Chapter 9

The Unshakable Foundation

A BUILDING IS ONLY as strong as the foundation it rests on. The same is true for faith. In a world where opinions shift with trends and morals bend under pressure, the believer's only unshakable foundation is the word of God. Jesus made this clear in Matt 7:24–27: those who hear his words and put them into practice are like a wise man who built his house on rock—when the storms came, it stood.

The Nature of the Foundation

The foundation of faith is not feelings, traditions, or even personal experiences but the unchanging truth of Scripture. Feelings can be misleading, traditions can be corrupted, and experiences can be misinterpreted, but God's word remains true in every generation. Psalm 119:89 declares, "Your word, LORD, is eternal; it stands firm in the heavens."

Why the Foundation Matters

- *Stability in Storms*—When trials come, only those grounded in God's truth will endure.

- *Clarity in Confusion*—God's word is a lamp to our feet and a light to our path (Ps 119:105).
- *Resistance to Deception*—False teachings crumble before those who know the truth.
- *Growth in Maturity*—Deep roots in Scripture enable believers to discern God's will in all circumstances.

Building on the Foundation

- *Learn the Word*—Regular study of Scripture is essential to strengthening your spiritual base.
- *Live the Word*—Truth must be applied, not merely known.
- *Defend the Word*—Be ready to give an answer for the hope within you.
- *Pass on the Word*—Teach and model biblical truth to the next generation.

Examples from Scripture

Joshua was commanded to meditate on God's law, day and night, so he would be careful to do everything written in it—and his leadership was marked by strength and success. The early church devoted themselves to the apostles' teaching, creating a unified, resilient community despite persecution. Even Jesus, in his humanity, resisted Satan's temptations by declaring, "It is written."[1]

The Danger of a Weak Foundation

When believers neglect the word, they become vulnerable to false doctrines and cultural compromise. A shallow foundation can

---

1. Matt 4:4, 7, 10; Luke 4:4, 8, 12.

support faith in fair weather, but it cannot withstand the floods of opposition.

Closing Reflection

In a time when the ground beneath many is shifting, the people of God must build on what cannot be moved. The storms will come—and may already be here—but those who stand on the rock of God's word will not be shaken. Our calling is not merely to admire the foundation but to live upon it, letting every decision, every conviction, and every hope rest firmly on the truth that endures forever.

Chapter 10

When the World Shifts Beneath Your Feet

Life has a way of shaking even the most stable ground. Cultures change, economies collapse, relationships fracture, and freedoms vanish. For those whose security depends on circumstances, such shifts can be devastating. But for those anchored in Christ, the ground may tremble without their faith collapsing.

The Reality of Shifting Times

Across history, God's people have faced sudden upheaval. The Israelites were taken into exile, the early church endured waves of persecution, and countless believers have watched their nations turn hostile toward the gospel. The Bible never promises that the world will remain steady; in fact, it warns that everything that can be shaken will be shaken (Heb 12:26–27).

Where Stability Comes From

- *God's Character*—His nature does not change with the headlines or the decades.

- *God's Word*—Truth remains truth whether accepted or rejected by the culture.
- *God's Presence*—In Christ, we are never alone, even when the world feels unfamiliar.
- *God's Kingdom*—Our ultimate home is unshakable, untouched by earthly turmoil.

Learning from Scripture's Witnesses

Daniel served faithfully under pagan kings whose laws opposed his faith. Jeremiah proclaimed truth to a nation on the brink of judgment. Paul wrote letters of encouragement from prison cells. Their strength was never rooted in stable governments or favorable conditions but in a God who reigns over history.

Practical Steps for Standing Firm in Unstable Times

- *Stay Grounded in Scripture*—When the world's moral compass spins wildly, return to the fixed point of God's word.
- *Strengthen Christian Community*—Isolation breeds fear; fellowship strengthens faith.
- *Keep an Eternal Perspective*—Earthly kingdoms rise and fall, but God's kingdom is forever.
- *Practice Daily Dependence*—Ask God for the grace to endure today, trusting him for tomorrow.

When God Uses the Shaking

Sometimes God allows instability to strip away false securities and refocus his people on what matters most. The shaking is not always a curse; it can be a mercy that drives us back to the Rock.

Closing Reflection

When the world shifts beneath your feet, you may feel fear, but you need not be moved from your foundation. The same God who walked with his people through exile, persecution, and every storm of history walks with you now. Stand firm, not because the ground is steady but because the One you stand on cannot be shaken.

Chapter 11

Discerning the Spirit of the Age

Every generation has its spirit—the dominant attitude, belief, or cultural current that shapes the way people think, feel, and live. The Bible calls it "the spirit of the world" (1 Cor 2:12) or "the spirit of the age" (Eph 2:2), referring to the invisible but powerful influence that pulls humanity away from God.

Understanding the Spirit of the Age

The Spirit of the Age is not just about politics, fashion, or technology; it is about the underlying values and assumptions that become so normal, most people never think to question them. In every era, these values subtly redefine right and wrong, truth and falsehood, even the definition of what it means to be human.

Biblical Example: Daniel in Babylon

When Daniel and his friends were taken to Babylon, they were immersed in a culture that sought to erase their identity. Their names were changed, their education was reshaped, and they were expected to serve a pagan king. Yet Daniel "resolved that he would not defile himself" (Dan 1:8). He discerned that accepting the king's food—offered to idols—was more than a meal; it was a spiritual compromise. Daniel's example shows that resisting the spirit of the age begins with the smallest acts of faithfulness.

How to Recognize It Today

- *It Redefines Truth*—What was once called sin is now celebrated as virtue.
- *It Normalizes Compromise*—Faith is tolerated only if it bends to cultural norms.
- *It Distracts with Noise*—Entertainment, outrage, and endless information drown out God's voice.
- *It Appeals to Pride*—Encouraging people to be "their own truth" rather than submit to God.

Tools for Discernment

- *Test Every Message by Scripture*—If an idea contradicts God's word, no matter how popular, it is not from him.
- *Watch for the Fruit*—Jesus said we would know a tree by its fruit. Does a cultural movement produce humility, love, and righteousness, or pride, division, and corruption?
- *Stay in God's Presence*—Discernment is sharpened when you are walking closely with him.
- *Seek Godly Counsel*—Isolated Christians are more easily deceived.

A Modern Case Study: The Idol of Self

In our day, one of the most dominant spirits of the age is the worship of self. It teaches that personal feelings define reality, that autonomy is the highest good, and that any moral standard that limits self-expression is oppressive. This is nothing new—it is the same lie the serpent told Eve: "You will be like God" (Gen 3:5). It sounds empowering, but it leads to emptiness, division, and ultimately, destruction.

The Call to Resist

Resisting the spirit of the age is not about nostalgia or clinging to the past. It is about standing on eternal truth when the tide of opinion turns against it. It is about speaking with grace and living with conviction, so that even those who oppose you cannot deny your integrity.

Closing Reflection

The spirit of the age will always change, but the Spirit of God will never change. If you know his voice, you will recognize every counterfeit. And if you walk in his truth, you will not just survive your generation, you will shine in it—like Daniel in Babylon, a living testimony that God's ways are higher, his truth unshakable, and his kingdom everlasting.

Chapter 12

Living as Light in the Darkness

Jesus said, "You are the light of the world. A city set on a hill cannot be hidden" (Matt 5:14). Light is not simply something we carry—it is what we are, because Christ, the true Light, dwells within us. In the world's darkest moments, the smallest flicker of that light can reveal a path, expose a lie, or ignite hope.

The Nature of Light

Throughout Scripture, light is more than brightness. It is purity (Ps 27:1), truth (John 8:12), and the very presence of God (Isa 60:1–2). Light separates from darkness, just as holiness separates from sin. And when Jesus calls us to shine, he is not asking for self-promotion—he is commanding us to reflect his own nature in how we live, speak, and love.

Historical Case Study: Dietrich Bonhoeffer

In 1930s Germany, the darkness of Nazi ideology seeped into every part of society, including the church. Many pastors compromised, adapting their sermons to align with state propaganda. But one young theologian, Dietrich Bonhoeffer, refused to let the light be dimmed. He helped form the Confessing Church, which openly rejected Hitler's attempt to redefine Christianity.[1] When others stayed silent, Bonhoeffer warned that silence in the face of evil is itself evil.

Even under threat of arrest, he continued to train pastors in underground seminaries. Captured in 1943, he spent two years in prison, writing letters that still inspire believers to stand firm.[2] Just weeks before Germany's surrender, Bonhoeffer was executed.[3] His life remains a testament that the cost of shining is great, but the reward is eternal.

Modern Parallel: Faith

Under surveillance in China today, in parts of China, the state monitors church gatherings with cameras, records attendees' identities, and even rewrites Scripture to fit political ideology. One altered passage replaces Jesus' words to the woman caught in adultery—"Let him who is without sin cast the first stone"[4]—with a distortion claiming she must be stoned to uphold the law. This twisting of truth is designed to align the gospel with authoritarian control.

Yet despite constant surveillance, believers gather in secret or under watchful eyes, singing softly, sharing the word from memory, and baptizing in hidden locations. Their light is not diminished by fear—it is sharpened by it. For them, being light means risking everything for the joy of following Christ.

How We Shine in Our Time

- *Live with Visible Integrity*—Be the same person in private as in public.

---

1. Metaxas, *Bonhoeffer*, 231–64.
2. Bethge, *Dietrich Bonhoeffer*, 747–810; Bonhoeffer, *Letters and Papers from Prison*.
3. Metaxas, *Bonhoeffer*, 524–30.
4. John 8:7.

- *Speak Truth with Grace*—Our words must cut through lies without wounding unnecessarily.
- *Serve Selflessly*—Light is most credible when it warms others.
- *Stay Rooted in Scripture*—Only God's word can fuel light that does not fade.
- *Refuse to Compromise*—Even small concessions to darkness can dim a witness.

The Unstoppable Power of Light

Darkness can threaten, intimidate, and even kill the messenger, but it cannot extinguish the light of Christ. Every generation has its Bonhoeffers, its faithful in China, its nameless saints who shine where they are planted. Their courage becomes a spark that ignites others.

A Call to the Reader

You may not face imprisonment or government surveillance, but you will face moments when silence is easier than truth. In those moments, remember: you are the city on a hill, the lamp on the stand. The world does not need more people who blend into the shadows—it needs disciples who carry the unfiltered light of Christ.

Your life can become a lighthouse in someone's storm, a beacon pointing to the safe harbor of God's grace. Let it be said of you, as it was of Bonhoeffer and of countless unnamed believers: they did not hide the light, even when the night was at its darkest.

Chapter 13

The Reward of Endurance

ENDURANCE IS NOT SIMPLY the act of holding on; it is the art of pressing forward when every force around you insists you should stop. In Scripture, endurance is always tied to faith, because it is faith that gives meaning to the struggle and direction to the journey.

The Biblical Call to Endure

James 1:12 declares, "Blessed is the one who perseveres under trial because, having stood the test, that person will receive the crown of life that the Lord has promised to those who love him." Endurance is not passive—it is active, resilient, and anchored in the unshakable promises of God. Hebrews 12:1-2 urges us to run "with perseverance the race marked out for us, fixing our eyes on Jesus, the pioneer and perfecter of faith." Endurance is not about survival for survival's sake; it is about finishing well.

Historical Example: William Wilberforce

In the late eighteenth and early nineteenth centuries, William Wilberforce fought tirelessly for the abolition of the British slave trade. For decades, he faced political resistance, personal attacks, and physical illness. Yet his faith in Christ fueled an unrelenting commitment to justice.[1] He introduced bill after bill, year after year, knowing each defeat was just another step toward inevitable victory.[2] In 1807, the slave trade was finally abolished,[3] and in 1833—just three days before his death—slavery itself was outlawed in the British Empire.[4] Wilberforce's life reminds us that endurance can reshape the moral landscape of nations.

Modern Parallel: Pastor Wang Yi of China

In December 2018, Pastor Wang Yi, leader of the Early Rain Covenant Church, was arrested for "inciting to subvert state power" simply for preaching the gospel without state approval.[5] Sentenced to nine years in prison, he wrote before his arrest that he was willing to lose his freedom and even his life to remain faithful to Christ.[6] From his cell, his witness continues to strengthen the faith of believers around the world.[7] His endurance is not in loud protest but in steadfast obedience, proving that true victory is measured in faithfulness, not circumstance.

The Spiritual Logic of Endurance

The enemy's greatest weapon is not always destruction—it is discouragement. If he can convince us to give up, he wins without a fight. Endurance strips that weapon from his hand. When believers refuse to bow, refuse to break, and refuse to retreat, they declare that God's promises are worth more than earthly comfort or safety.

1. Wilberforce, *Practical View of Christianity*.
2. Hague, *William Wilberforce*, 291–350.
3. Hochschild, *Bury the Chains*, 330–47.
4. Belmonte, *William Wilberforce*, 253–61.
5. BBC News, "China's Pre-Christmas Crackdown Raises Alarm"; The Guardian, "China Jails Underground Pastor."
6. Yi. "My Declaration of Faithful Disobedience."
7. International Christian Concern, "Imprisoned Chinese Pastor's Church."

The Reward of Endurance

Revelation 2:10 offers a startlingly beautiful promise: "Be faithful, even to the point of death, and I will give you life as your victor's crown." Endurance is not wasted energy—it is an investment into eternity.

How We Cultivate Endurance

- *Remember the Witnesses*—Surround yourself with the stories of those who have gone before (Heb 12:1).
- *Feed on the Word*—Scripture is the fuel for perseverance.
- *Pray Without Ceasing*—Prayer keeps us connected to the source of strength.
- *Lean on the Body of Christ*—We endure best when we endure together.
- *Keep Eternity in View*—Temporary suffering cannot outweigh eternal glory.

A Vision for the Enduring Church

Endurance is not glamorous. It rarely makes headlines. It is often lonely, unseen, and misunderstood. But it is the heartbeat of every revival, the foundation of every victory, and the thread that ties the church's story from the martyrs of Rome to the underground churches of today.

If the church of tomorrow is to shine in the darkness, it will be because the church of today chose to endure—through cultural hostility, through personal trials, through spiritual droughts. The crown of life awaits not the swiftest runner nor the loudest voice but the one who, by God's grace, did not quit.

So, stand. Stand when the night feels endless. Stand when your prayers seem unanswered. Stand when the cost feels unbearable. For in the economy of heaven, every act of endurance is a step toward the moment when you will hear the words that make it all worthwhile: "Well done, good and faithful servant . . . enter into the joy of your Master."[8]

---

8. Matt 25:21.

PART 5

The Global Battlefield of Ideas

Chapter 1

The Global Battlefield of Ideas

HUMAN HISTORY CAN BE read as a series of wars—not only those fought with weapons, but those fought with ideas. Armies may conquer lands, but it is ideas that conquer minds, shape laws, inspire revolutions, and determine what a civilization will call "good" and "evil." From the first campfires to the digital age, every culture has wrestled with the same unyielding questions: Who are we? Why are we here? What does it mean to live well? What happens when we die?

The answers have never been uniform. In every age, competing visions of truth have stood against one another like rival kingdoms—some appealing to divine revelation, others to human reason, and others to the cold indifference of nature. Together, they form a battlefield that stretches from the temples of ancient Mesopotamia to the lecture halls of modern universities, from the shrines of distant mountains to the glowing screens in our pockets.

The Human Quest for Meaning

Our species has an unrelenting need to interpret reality. We build stories about the cosmos and our place in it, because without them, life feels like chaos. Ancient Egyptians saw the sun's daily rise as the journey of a god across the sky, a cosmic drama of order overcoming chaos. Greek philosophers sought harmony through reason, believing the universe could be understood through mathematics and logic. Eastern mystics taught that ultimate reality was beyond words, to be encountered in stillness and self-denial. The modern West has often looked to science as the final arbiter, imagining that enough data could one day answer every question.

Each of these worldviews was born in a cultural soil, watered by its history, and shaped by its fears and hopes. Yet all of them—from the most religious to the most secular—are attempting the same thing: to explain reality, justify morality, and give meaning to life.

The Great Families of Worldview

For all their variety, most human belief systems fall into a few broad families:

1. The Theistic Vision—God or gods as the source of life, meaning, and moral order.

    - Ancient Judaism, Christianity, Islam, and many indigenous traditions share this starting point.
    - Strength: Offers a personal, relational source of morality and purpose.
    - Limitation: Disagreement over which revelation is true, and how it should be interpreted.

2. The Naturalistic Vision—Nature is all there is, governed by impersonal laws.

    - Modern atheism, scientific materialism, and secular humanism fit here.
    - Strength: Relies on observable evidence and measurable phenomena.
    - Limitation: Struggles to explain consciousness, morality, and meaning without borrowing from theistic concepts.

3. The Pantheistic/Mystical Vision—God and the universe are one; reality is ultimately spiritual but impersonal.
   - This perspective is found in Hinduism, some strands of Buddhism, and modern New Age thought.
   - Strength: Emphasizes unity, transcendence, and inner transformation.
   - Limitation: Often dissolves personal identity and moral absolutes into ambiguity.
4. The Syncretic Vision—This is a blending of elements from multiple systems, adapted to personal preference or political need.
   - This pattern is common in empires, multicultural societies, and increasingly in the postmodern West.
   - Strength: Flexible and inclusive.
   - Limitation: Risks creating a worldview that is comforting but incoherent.

The Science Factor

In the modern age, science has become the dominant voice in the public square—often stepping beyond its natural boundaries of observation and experiment into the realm of metaphysics. Discoveries in cosmology, quantum physics, and genetics have transformed our understanding of the universe. Yet the more we learn, the more we uncover questions that science alone cannot answer.

Cosmology tells us the universe had a beginning—but not *why* there was a beginning, or why there is something rather than nothing. Quantum mechanics reveals that the foundations of reality behave in ways that defy classical logic—hinting at deeper layers of order we do not yet understand. Biology explains how life adapts and survives—but not why conscious beings would ponder morality, beauty, or eternity.

The irony is that science, when honest, has expanded the mystery rather than eliminated it.

History as a Laboratory of Truth

History offers its own verdicts. Civilizations rise and fall not only by the strength of their armies but by the truthfulness and durability of their ideas. Empires built on cruelty eventually devour themselves. Societies that honor justice and self-sacrifice tend to flourish—at least until they forget the principles that made them strong.

From Rome's roads and laws to the Islamic Golden Age's scholarship to the Enlightenment's emphasis on reason, humanity has seen periods where certain ideas transformed the world. Yet every such era also carried within it the seeds of its decline—because every worldview must answer not only the question of meaning but the problem of human nature.

The Coming Convergence

Today, the battlefield has shifted again. We live in an era where ideas travel faster than armies, where a philosophy born in one corner of the world can be in every smartphone within hours. This interconnectedness has not led to unity but to a global collision of narratives. Competing truths jostle for dominance—sometimes peacefully, sometimes with the force of law, and sometimes at the point of a sword.

Technology has amplified this battle, but it has not resolved it. Artificial intelligence, genetic engineering, and digital surveillance have raised new ethical questions for which ancient wisdom is still urgently relevant. The question is no longer whether humanity will be guided by an overarching truth—but which truth will claim the future?

Why this Battlefield Matters

The "battlefield of ideas" is not an academic metaphor. It is the ground on which our laws are made, our wars are justified, our children are educated, and our hopes are built. What you believe about reality will determine how you live, how you treat others, and what kind of world you leave behind.

In the chapters ahead, we will walk through this battlefield—not as tourists but as truth-seekers. We will examine the world's most influential belief systems, their strengths and weaknesses, their promises and their failures. We will see where science and faith intersect, where they diverge, and where both must bow to a reality greater than themselves.

Because in the end, this is not just about ideas. It is about destiny. And destiny is shaped by what we believe to be true.

Chapter 2

The Great Contenders
How the World Seeks Truth

Across the centuries, humanity's search for truth has crystallized into several major belief systems. These are not just abstract ideas; they are living traditions, woven into the cultures, laws, and identities of billions. They inspire the highest acts of compassion and the darkest acts of cruelty. Each claims, in its own way, to tell the truth about reality—and each must be examined not only for what it promises but for whether it delivers.

Christianity—The God Who Came Down

At the heart of Christianity lies a staggering claim: that God himself entered human history in the person of Jesus Christ, not as a distant messenger but as Emmanuel—"God with us." In the Gospels, Jesus does not merely point toward truth; he identifies himself as "the way, the truth, and the life."[1] Unlike other faiths, where the path to God is a set of rules or disciplines, Christianity declares that the path is a Person—one who lived without sin, died for the sins of others, and rose again to break the power of death.

---

1. John 14:6.

The Great Contenders

From the first-century house churches of Jerusalem to underground congregations in modern China, Christians have proclaimed a gospel of grace: salvation as a gift, not a wage. Critics see in this a dangerous moral looseness; believers see it as the only hope for a fallen humanity. The historical question is whether Jesus truly rose from the dead—for if he did, Christianity's foundation is unshakable. If he did not, its walls collapse.

Islam—Submission to the Will of Allah

Emerging in seventh-century Arabia, Islam presents itself as the final, uncorrupted revelation from God, delivered through the Prophet Muhammad. The Qur'an acknowledges figures from Jewish and Christian Scripture, including Jesus, but reframes them in a way that denies his divinity and his crucifixion. Central to Islam is the concept of *tawhid*—the absolute oneness of God—and the call to submit entirely to his will.[2]

Islamic civilization has produced vast empires, intricate legal systems, and rich philosophical traditions. Its unity is remarkable, but its diversity is often underestimated. From Sufi mystics to strict literalists, interpretations vary widely. The question it faces is whether its vision of God—transcendent yet impersonal—can offer the same intimacy and assurance found in the God of the gospel.

Hinduism—The Endless Cycle

Hinduism is less a single creed than a vast spiritual ecosystem, with roots reaching back more than three thousand years. Its sacred texts speak of a universe in constant cycle—birth, death, and rebirth—governed by *karma*, the law of moral cause and effect. The ultimate goal is liberation (*moksha*), to escape the cycle and be united with *Brahman*, the infinite divine reality.[3]

---

2. Esposito, *Islam*, 12–20; Armstrong, *Islam*, 3–15.
3. Flood, *Introduction to Hinduism*, 86–105.

The beauty of Hinduism lies in its adaptability, its embrace of many paths—devotion, meditation, ethical living. Yet its very openness can also blur the lines between truth and myth, between the personal and the impersonal. For the Christian, the striking difference is that in the gospel, salvation is not escape from the world but the renewal of it.

Buddhism—The Path of Liberation

Buddhism began as a reform movement within Hinduism, sparked by the awakening of Siddhartha Gautama—the Buddha—in the fifth century BC. Rejecting the authority of the Vedas, the Buddha taught that suffering arises from desire, and that liberation comes by following the Noble Eightfold Path toward detachment and enlightenment.

Buddhism offers profound insight into the nature of human dissatisfaction. It is a path of discipline, mindfulness, and compassion. Yet, for all its wisdom, it leaves unanswered the question of ultimate justice—for if there is no personal God, who guarantees that evil will be judged and good rewarded?

Judaism—The Covenant People

Judaism is the root from which both Christianity and Islam historically sprang. It tells the story of a God who chose a people, entered into covenant with them, and revealed his law through Moses and the prophets. Its hope is anchored in the promises of God—promises that, according to Christians, are fulfilled in Jesus, the Jewish Messiah.

For two millennia, Judaism has endured exile, persecution, and dispersion, yet has maintained its identity through faith, law, and tradition. The central question is whether the Messiah has already come—or whether he is yet to appear.

The Great Contenders

Secular Humanism—Man as the Measure

In the modern West, a growing number embrace a worldview without God. Secular humanism sees humanity as capable of defining morality and purpose without reference to the divine. Science, reason, and human rights become the guiding lights.

This vision has inspired great social progress—yet it is haunted by unanswered questions. If morality is human-made, why should it be binding on anyone? If life is a cosmic accident, why does justice matter? Without a transcendent reference point, the moral law risks dissolving into preference.

A Clash of Absolutes

These belief systems are not merely private opinions; they are competing claims about reality itself. They cannot all be equally true, for they contradict one another at their core. Either God is personal or impersonal. Either Jesus is the Son of God or he is not. Either the universe is cyclical, or it is moving toward a final destiny.

In the chapters that follow, we will not treat these claims lightly. We will examine them in their historical, philosophical, and spiritual dimensions—asking of each what it asks of us: Will you trust this vision of reality enough to stake your life on it?

The battlefield of ideas is no less fierce here than in politics or war. For the victor in this struggle will shape the soul of the future.

Chapter 3

Testing the Claims

In chapter 2, we surveyed the great contenders for humanity's allegiance—the major world religions and philosophies that have shaped civilizations. Now, we must do what few dare: test their claims—not merely by sentiment or tradition but by the hard edge of evidence, logic, and lived reality.

Christianity—A Claim Anchored in History

Christianity's central claim is not an abstract teaching but an event: the resurrection of Jesus. As the apostle Paul reminds us, the resurrection stands at the center of the Christian proclamation—not because history creates truth, but because the resurrection is the historical expression of who Christ truly is. The historical question therefore turns to the reliability of the Gospel accounts, the transformation of the disciples, the empty tomb, and the birth of the early church in the face of persecution.

No other major religion makes its entire credibility hinge on a verifiable point in history. Archaeology continues to affirm the cultural and geographical details in the Gospels.[1] While skeptics propose alternative theories—mass hallucinations, stolen

---

1. Charlesworth, *Jesus and Archaeology*; McRay, *Archaeology and the New Testament*; Evans, *Jesus and His World*.

bodies—none fully account for the breadth of evidence. Christianity stands or falls on a question that is both testable and deeply personal: Did Jesus rise from the dead?

Islam

The Uncorrupted Revelation? Islam claims to be the final, unaltered word of God, correcting errors in the Torah and the Gospels. This is a testable claim. Textual criticism shows the New Testament we have today is virtually identical to what existed centuries before Muhammad. The Qur'an affirms the authority of the earlier scriptures in some verses, yet contradicts their central message in others—particularly regarding the crucifixion.

Historically, Islam spread with remarkable speed, but often under the shadow of military power. Its moral vision has inspired devotion and justice in many, but it faces the philosophical challenge of explaining divine justice without the cross—without God himself paying the debt of sin.

Hinduism

The problem of endless cycles Hinduism's promise is liberation from the cycle of birth and rebirth through union with *Brahman*. But how can one know with certainty that such liberation is real? The cyclical view of time makes historical validation almost impossible; truth becomes experiential rather than evidential. For seekers weary of suffering, this may be enough. But for those asking whether reality itself can be known and tested, the path grows less clear.

Moreover, *karma* offers a kind of moral order, but it can also justify passivity toward suffering—seeing it as deserved rather than as a wrong to be righted.

Buddhism—Noble but Incomplete

Buddhism offers profound diagnosis: suffering is rooted in desire. Its prescription—the Noble Eightfold Path—fosters discipline and compassion. Yet it offers no ultimate assurance that justice will be done. Without a personal God, the universe has no moral guarantor. The end of suffering may come, but so might the end of meaning itself.

Judaism—Waiting for the Promise

Judaism's claim rests on God's covenant and the yet-to-come Messiah. The test here is historical and prophetic: Has the Messiah already fulfilled the prophecies, or are they still to come? The Hebrew Scriptures contain messianic descriptions—a suffering servant, a bringer of peace, one from the line of David. Christians argue that Jesus fulfilled these in ways no other figure has. If he did not, the wait continues. If he did, then the covenant reaches its intended goal in him.

Secular Humanism—Morality

Secular humanism asserts that morality and meaning can exist without God. The test here is philosophical: If humans are the sole authors of morality, then morality is ultimately subjective. What one culture calls good, another may call evil. Science can tell us what is, but not what ought to be. The humanist vision of progress often borrows moral capital from religious traditions it claims to transcend.

This leads to what I call the Common Test: every worldview must answer three questions: Is it internally consistent? Does it fit the facts of history and experience? And does it offer a hope that satisfies both mind and heart?

When these tests are applied, many systems offer fragments of truth but fall short of the whole. Some excel in ethics

Testing the Claims

but falter in evidence. Others provide comfort but collapse under contradiction.

Christianity's uniqueness lies in combining historical verifiability, philosophical coherence, and a hope that is both personal and universal.

In the chapters ahead, we will not stop at theory. We will press deeper, into the lived consequences of these beliefs—for ideas do not remain on paper. They shape laws, cultures, and destinies. And in that realm, the test becomes ultimate: not only "Is this true?" but "Will this truth set us free?"

Chapter 4

Christianity

The Claim and the Proof

Origins

The life that changed history two thousand years ago in a remote corner of the Roman Empire, a carpenter from Nazareth began teaching, healing, and proclaiming a message unlike any the world had heard. He spoke with the authority of God himself, yet without the trappings of political or military power. Jesus of Nazareth's ministry lasted barely three years, yet it redefined history.

The early Christian movement did not arise in a vacuum. It was the culmination of centuries of Hebrew prophecy, law, and covenant—a divine story stretching from Abraham through the prophets to its fulfillment in Christ. From the outset, Christianity claimed not to be a new religion but the completion of God's revelation to Israel.

Core Beliefs

The core of Christianity is the gospel—the "good news" that God became man, lived a sinless life, died for our sins, and rose again to

Christianity

offer eternal life to all who believe. This is not merely moral guidance; it is a rescue mission. Grace, not human achievement, is the foundation. The relationship with God is not earned; it is given.

The resurrection is central. Without it, Christianity collapses into moral philosophy. With it, Christianity stands as God's definitive intervention in human history.

Historical Evidence—Verifiable Claims

The Christian faith is uniquely anchored to historical events. The crucifixion of Jesus is one of the most well-attested facts of ancient history, recorded not only in the Gospels but in Roman and Jewish sources such as Tacitus and Josephus.[1] The resurrection is supported by multiple independent accounts, the radical transformation of the disciples, and the explosive growth of the early church despite persecution.

Archaeology has repeatedly confirmed the accuracy of the New Testament's cultural and geographical details. The Dead Sea Scrolls, early manuscripts such as Codex Sinaiticus, and thousands of other textual witnesses show a New Testament text stable and reliable over centuries.

Fulfilled Prophecy

The signature of God centuries before Christ, Hebrew prophets foretold a Messiah who would be born in Bethlehem (Mic 5:2), enter Jerusalem on a donkey (Zech 9:9), be betrayed for thirty pieces of silver (Zech 11:12–13), suffer and die for the sins of others (Isa 53), and rise again (Ps 16:10). Jesus fulfills these prophecies in ways that defy coincidence.

No other religious founder arrives on the stage of history with such a prophetic resume.

---

1. Tacitus, *Annals* 15.44; Josephus, *Jewish Antiquities* 18.3.3, 20.9.1.

Philosophical Strength—Coherence and Clarity

Christianity presents a worldview in which morality is rooted in the character of God, meaning is found in relationship with him, and hope is grounded in his promises. It uniquely resolves the tension between justice and mercy: at the cross, God's justice is satisfied and his mercy extended.

It answers the deepest human questions:

Origin—We are created in the image of God.

Meaning—We exist to know and love him.

Morality—Right and wrong flow from his unchanging nature.

Destiny—Eternal life with God for those who receive his grace, restored to the fullness of what humanity was meant to be.

Impact on the World—The world is transformed as God's people embody his goodness, justice, and love in every sphere of life.

Across Centuries

From its beginnings, Christianity transformed lives—tax collectors became generous, persecutors became apostles, and broken communities became centers of compassion. It inspired the abolition of slavery, the founding of hospitals, the defense of human rights, and the elevation of women and children in societies where they were undervalued.

Art, science, law, and education all bear the marks of Christian influence. The belief that the universe is orderly and knowable fueled the scientific revolution. The conviction that all people are equal before God undergirded movements for justice and human dignity.

The Living Testimony—Evidence in Every Generation

Christianity's truth claim is not locked in the past. Around the world, millions testify to lives transformed by Christ today—from drug addicts set free to persecuted believers who forgive their oppressors. The power of the gospel continues to bring light into darkness.

The resurrection is not just an ancient event; it is a present reality in the lives of those who follow him. Christianity's enduring strength lies in this living testimony: that Jesus Christ is the same yesterday, today, and forever.

In the chapters ahead, we will hold other worldviews to the same tests: historical credibility, philosophical coherence, and transformative power. Only then can we see, without prejudice or preconception, where truth ultimately resides.

Chapter 5

Islam

The Claim and the Challenge

Origins and History: From the Desert to an Empire

In the early seventh century, in the city of Mecca, a merchant named Muhammad claimed to have received a revelation from God through the Angel Jibril (Gabriel) while meditating in a cave on Mount Hira. These experiences, recorded over the next two decades, became the Qur'an, Islam's holy book. Muhammad began preaching monotheism in a polytheistic society, facing opposition from the Quraysh tribe before eventually migrating to Medina, where he became both a spiritual and political leader.[1]

Within a century of Muhammad's death, Islam had expanded through military conquest across the Middle East, North Africa, and parts of Europe and Asia. This rapid spread was as much a political and cultural movement as a religious one, shaping entire civilizations.[2]

---

1. Esposito, *Islam*, 81–95; Peters, *Islam*, 110–35; Armstrong, *Muhammad*, 25–85.

2. Donner, *Muhammad and the Believers*, 1–75, 121–70; Kennedy, *Great Arab Conquests*.

Core Beliefs

The Qur'an, the Pillars, and the Path: Islam's core beliefs center on the absolute oneness of God (Allah), the authority of the Qur'an as the final revelation, and Muhammad as the last and greatest prophet. The Five Pillars define Muslim practice:[3]

1. *Shahada*—Profession of faith: "There is no god but Allah, and Muhammad is the messenger of Allah."
2. *Salat*—Ritual prayer five times a day
3. *Zakat*—Giving to charity
4. *Sawm*—Fasting during Ramadan
5. *Hajj*—Pilgrimage to Mecca

The Qur'an is supplemented by the Hadith—collections of Muhammad's sayings and actions—which form the basis of Islamic law (Sharia). Salvation in Islam is achieved through faith in Allah, righteous deeds, and Allah's mercy, with the balance of one's good and bad deeds determining one's fate in the afterlife.

Historical Evidence—The Witness Problem

The historical challenge for Islam lies in the origin of its central claim: Muhammad's reception of the Qur'an. Unlike Christianity, whose defining events (Jesus' public ministry, crucifixion, resurrection) were witnessed by many and recorded by multiple sources, Muhammad's first revelation occurred alone in a cave. No one saw or heard the angel Jibril except Muhammad himself.

The Qur'an provides no independent eyewitness testimony to verify the divine origin of these revelations. Even Muhammad's own contemporaries doubted his claims,[4] accusing him of being a

---

3. Esposito, *Islam*, 3–40; Peters, *Islam*, 110–35; Armstrong, *Islam*.
4. Qur'an 25:4–5.

poet,[5] a sorcerer,[6] or influenced by others.[7] Early Islamic sources confirm that Muhammad initially feared he was possessed.[8]

In stark contrast, Christianity's core claim—the resurrection—was attested by multiple independent witnesses, hostile observers, physical evidence, and proclaimed in the same city where it happened within weeks of the event.

Philosophical Consistency—Testing the Qur'an's Claims

The Qur'an affirms that previous scriptures—the Torah and the Gospels—were given by God, yet also claims they were corrupted. This raises a problem: if God's earlier revelations could be corrupted beyond recognition, what assurance is there that the Qur'an has not suffered the same fate? Historical manuscript evidence for the Bible, including thousands of early copies, far exceeds that for the Qur'an,[9] which underwent standardization under Caliph Uthman, with variant readings destroyed.[10]

Additionally, the Qur'an presents conflicting portrayals of Jesus: a prophet who did miracles, born of a virgin, and honored by God—yet not crucified and certainly not divine. This selective affirmation of the gospel leaves Islam in tension with its own acknowledgment of Jesus' unique status.

Impact on Society—Civilization and Control

Islamic civilization produced significant contributions in science, mathematics, medicine, and architecture, particularly during the Golden Age. However, its political-religious unity has also

5. Qur'an 21:5.
6. Qur'an 74:24.
7. Qur'an 16:103.
8. Ishaq, *Sirat Rasul Allah*, 106–7; *Sahih al-Bukhari* 1.3.
9. Mustafa al-Azami, *History of the Qur'ānic Text*, 95–150; Cook, *Koran*, 65–79; Reynolds, *Qur'an in Its Historial Context*.
10. *Sahih al-Bukhari*, 61.510–11; Burton, *Collection of the Qur'an*, 111–43; Donner, *Muhammad and the Believers*, 96–110.

been marked by strict control, suppression of dissent, and legal structures that limit freedom of religion and expression. In many Muslim-majority nations today, conversion from Islam is punishable by death or imprisonment.

While Christianity spread primarily through witness, service, and martyrdom in its first centuries, Islam's expansion was often tied to political power and military conquest. The result is a faith that has been deeply intertwined with governance from its inception.

The Gospel Test

The missing proof when tested against the standard of public evidence, philosophical coherence, and transformative grace, Islam faces a decisive challenge. Its foundation rests entirely on the solitary experiences of one man, unverifiable by independent witnesses, and later enforced by political and military means.

The gospel, by contrast, offers an open invitation to "Come and see," grounded in verifiable history, fulfilled prophecy, and a God who entered the human story, not as a conqueror but as a servant.

In the next chapters, we will examine other worldviews with the same scrutiny—not to demean but to discern where truth ultimately resides, and why the gospel of Jesus Christ stands alone as the light that no darkness can overcome.

Chapter 6

Hinduism

Hierarchy of Men or the Image of God?

HINDUISM, ONE OF THE world's oldest religions, offers a vast tapestry of gods, rituals, and philosophies. Yet beneath its spiritual diversity lies one of history's most rigid social structures: the caste system.

The caste system, deeply intertwined with Hindu tradition, divides society into strict hereditary classes:

1. *Brahmins*—the priests and scholars, considered the highest and most "pure"
2. *Kshatriyas*—warriors and rulers
3. *Vaishyas*—merchants and farmers
4. *Shudras*—laborers and service workers
5. *Dalits* ("Untouchables")—historically deemed so impure that they fell outside the system entirely, tasked with the most degrading work and often shunned from public life

This hierarchy, traditionally justified as divinely ordained, has shaped Indian society for centuries. The injustice is not only historical; reports still emerge today of caste-based violence, exclusion from education, denial of temple entry, and even murder for crossing caste boundaries. In rural India, caste segregation can determine where a person lives, what water they may drink, and whom they may marry.[1]

The moral issue is stark: the caste system assigns value to human beings based on birth, not character or actions. It tells a child from a *Dalit* family that they are inherently less worthy than a child born to a *Brahmin* household. No merit, no repentance, no service can change one's caste in traditional Hindu belief.

Contrast this with the foundation of the Christian worldview. From the very first chapter of the Bible, the dignity of every human is declared: "So God created mankind in his own image, in the image of God he created them; male and female he created them" (Gen 1:27).

The worth of a human being is not determined by birth, wealth, or social status but by the fact that we bear the image of God. In Christ, this principle is expanded to abolish all human hierarchies before God: "There is neither Jew nor Gentile, neither slave nor free, nor is there male and female, for you are all one in Christ Jesus" (Gal 3:28).

History bears witness to the transformative power of this truth. When Christianity took root in societies built on rigid hierarchies—whether Rome's class system, medieval Europe's feudal order, or the racial segregation of the modern era—it planted seeds that would grow into movements for equality. While Christians have not always lived up to this calling, the moral vision that every human soul is equally valuable has repeatedly overturned entrenched systems of oppression.

Where the Hindu caste system demands separation, the gospel calls for fellowship. Where caste insists on purity by exclusion, Christ offers holiness through love. And while Hinduism teaches that one's social position is the result of past-life *karma*, Christianity declares that in Christ, anyone can be made new—no past sin, no inherited status, can separate us from the love of God.

---

1. Human Rights Watch, "They Say We're Dirty"; Amnesty International, "India 2024"; Dirks, *Castes of Mind*, 3–40, 247–90; Jodhka, *Caste in Contemporary India*.

Today, caste-based discrimination is officially illegal in India, yet it persists in hidden and open ways. Reports from human rights organizations tell of *Dalits* being denied access to wells, segregated in schools, and subjected to violence for challenging caste boundaries.[2] In contrast, many Christian communities in India actively work to dismantle these barriers, welcoming people of all castes into equal fellowship, running schools that educate *Dalit* children alongside others, and offering a vision of dignity that transcends birth.[3]

The choice between these visions is not merely religious; it is profoundly human. One tells you that your birth defines your destiny. The other tells you that your Creator does.

---

2. Barbour et al., "Hidden Apartheid"; Human Rights Watch, "They Say We're Dirty"; Amnesty International, "India 2024"; Jodhka, *Caste in Contemporary India*; Citizens for Justice and Peace, "Everyday Atrocity"; GFoD, "Communities Discriminated on Work"; International Dalit Solidarity Network. "Dalit Women"; Nandakumar, Prathima. "Lives, Buried"; Das and Mehta, "Poverty and Social Exclusion."

3. Kim and Kim, *History of Korean Christianity*, 185–200; Bergunder, *South Indian Pentecostal Movement*, 120–40; Barbour et al., "Hidden Apartheid"; Robinson, *Christians of India*, 210–40; World Vision India, "Child Wellbeing Report 2019"; Selvaraj and Marianathan, "Towards a New Dawn."

Chapter 7

Buddhism

The Silence of Nirvana vs. the Voice of God

BUDDHISM IS ONE OF the world's most admired religions, often praised for its peaceful image, meditative practices, and emphasis on compassion. Founded by Siddhartha Gautama, the Buddha, in the fifth to fourth century BC, it emerged as a response to the suffering and injustice he observed in the world.

Its heart lies in the Four Noble Truths:[1]

1. Life is suffering (*dukkha*)
2. Suffering arises from craving (*tanha*),
3. Suffering can be overcome,
4. The path to its cessation is the Eightfold Path—right understanding, right intention, right speech, right action, right livelihood, right effort, right mindfulness, and right concentration

On the surface, this seems noble and universally applicable. The recognition that life is filled with pain is not unique to Buddhism—it is a truth all humans face. But the way Buddhism

---

1. Rahula, *What the Buddha Taught*, 16–45; Keown, *Buddhism*, 31–52. Robinson and Johnson, *Buddhist Religion*, 34–48.

addresses it reveals the first great difference with Christianity. For the Buddhist, suffering is best ended by detaching from desire, letting go of all clinging until there is no self left to be hurt. The end goal is Nirvana—a state beyond all distinctions, beyond personal existence, beyond even consciousness as we know it.

The Christian answer to suffering is entirely different. It does not seek escape from existence, but the redemption of existence. In Christianity, the problem is not desire itself but disordered desire—when love is misdirected away from God. Jesus does not call us to annihilate the self but to transform it: "I have come that they may have life, and have it to the full" (John 10:10).

The Logical Gaps in Buddhism

While Buddhism offers a moral path, it rests on a worldview without a Creator, without an absolute moral lawgiver. If there is no personal God, moral principles become descriptive rather than prescriptive—they may help life function smoothly, but they are not binding in the ultimate sense. Without a transcendent source of morality, concepts like compassion and justice are preferences, not obligations.

Buddhism also teaches *anatta*, the doctrine that there is no enduring self. This raises a logical problem: If there is no "you" in any ultimate sense, then who suffers now, and who reaps the karmic consequences in the next life? If the self is an illusion, then the whole framework of *karma* collapses into incoherence.

Christianity, in contrast, affirms the reality of the self—created in the image of God, endowed with dignity, and made for eternal life. The Christian can meaningfully say "I" because there is a God who knows us personally and eternally.

Historical and Cultural Realities

It is tempting to idealize Buddhist cultures as naturally peaceful. Yet, history tells a more complex story. In countries such as Myanmar and Sri Lanka, Buddhist monks have at times supported ethnic violence and political oppression.[2] Even in times of peace, Buddhist societies have not always dismantled systems of injustice—because their framework focuses on personal liberation from suffering rather than on transforming society in the light of divine justice.[3]

By contrast, the Christian worldview—especially when faithfully applied—has birthed movements for human equality, abolition of slavery, and defense of the weak. This flows directly from the belief that every person is of equal worth, made in the image of God and accountable to him.

The Voice of God vs. the Silence of Nirvana

The ultimate goal of Buddhism is silence—the quiet extinguishing of the self into Nirvana. The ultimate goal of Christianity is the voice of God, calling his children into eternal relationship, joy, and purpose. One seeks an escape from the cycle of suffering; the other promises the renewal of all creation.

If the heart longs for love, justice, and meaning, the Christian message offers what Buddhism cannot: not just the absence of suffering but the presence of perfect love. In Christ, suffering is not merely ended—it is transformed into glory.

Ultimately, the choice is between an impersonal cessation and an eternal embrace, between the fading out of the self and the full flowering of the self in the presence of God, between the silence of Nirvana and the voice that spoke the universe into being.

Buddhism's recognition of pride as the root of suffering is one of its most insightful truths, and in this, it agrees with Christianity's teaching that pride was the first and oldest sin—the sin that caused Lucifer's fall. However, Buddhism's proposed solution—to dissolve the self entirely and fade into nonexistence—misses a

---

2. International Crisis Group, "Dark Side of Transition"; Human Rights Watch, "All You Can Do"; Walton, *Buddhism, Politics and Political Thought*; Tambiah, *Buddhism Betrayed?*; DeVotta, "Buddhist Nationalism and Ethnic Conflict."

3. Spiro, *Buddhism and Society*; Gombrich, *Theravada Buddhism*.

crucial truth. The self, as created by God, is inherently good; the problem is not that we exist but that our will is misaligned with God's. Christianity does not seek to erase the self but to redeem and transform it, restoring it to its intended glory through humility, repentance, and love. In Christ, the believer's identity is not obliterated but perfected—made whole, reconciled, and brought into eternal relationship with God. This offers a far more coherent and hopeful vision than the Buddhist aim of Nirvana, because it affirms the eternal worth of the person while still confronting and overcoming pride.

Chapter 8

Judaism

The Root of the Story

JUDAISM STANDS AS THE root from which Christianity grew. Without its soil of covenant, prophecy, and divine law, the gospel would be incomprehensible. To grasp the full meaning of Christ's life, death, and resurrection, a Christian must first become Jewish in spirit—not in ritual obligation but in understanding. The Old Testament was written by Jews, for Jews, in a Jewish world. Its language, customs, and symbols are the context that makes prophecy come alive.

Daniel's visions, Isaiah's servant songs, and the psalms of David were not random religious texts—they were a continuous narrative building toward the arrival of the Messiah. When Christians read these without understanding their original frame, much is missed. But when read as the Jewish people first heard them, the gospel is illuminated in its fullness. Daniel's seventy weeks (Dan 9) point precisely to the time of Christ's coming. Isaiah 53 describes in stunning detail the suffering servant who bears the sins of the world. Psalm 22 mirrors the crucifixion scene centuries before Rome perfected crucifixion as a method of execution.

This is why Christians, in pursuit of full knowledge, must be Jewish in spirit first—not to dwell in the old covenant but to understand the heart of God's story from its beginning. Only then can one appreciate how Jesus fulfills—not abolishes—the Law and the Prophets.

The same logic applies to Muslims. The Qur'an claims to confirm the Torah and the Gospels, so by its own claim, one must first know and test those Scriptures before accepting the Qur'an's authority. If the Torah and Gospels are not understood, one cannot truly assess whether the Qur'an upholds or contradicts them. Therefore, the path to truth is not to begin at the Qur'an but to walk the path of Abraham, Moses, and the prophets, and then encounter Christ.

Of all three Abrahamic faiths, only Christianity completes the arc. Judaism holds the promise; Christianity delivers the fulfillment; Islam comes later, altering the story it claims to preserve. Without the Jewish root, Christianity would lose its prophetic foundation; without Christianity, Judaism would be an unfinished symphony.

This is the chain of revelation: the Law and the Prophets prepare the way, the Messiah fulfills the promise, and the Spirit brings the full truth to the world. To know the end, you must understand the beginning. That is why the first step in knowing Christ fully is to be Jewish in spirit—standing where the prophets stood, seeing as they saw, and recognizing the Messiah they long awaited.

At the threshold of synthesis, as we stand at the close of our exploration of the world's major religions, it is clear that humanity's quest for truth is as old as our existence. From the temples of ancient India to the synagogues of Jerusalem, from the chanting halls of Buddhist monasteries to the mosques that echo with the call to prayer, mankind has sought to answer the same questions: Who are we? Why are we here? What is the purpose of life, and what lies beyond death?

These questions are not trivial—they form the very fabric of human consciousness. Across cultures and centuries, civilizations have constructed systems of belief to give shape to the unknown, to clothe mystery with meaning. In every tradition, we find glimpses of truth—sparks that testify to a deeper reality beyond our immediate perception. And yet, the paths diverge, and the answers vary—sometimes subtly, sometimes radically.

Hinduism, with its layered philosophies and ancient rituals, teaches the soul's journey through many lives. Buddhism seeks liberation from suffering through the quiet extinguishing of desire. Judaism holds steadfast to the covenant between God and his chosen people. Islam calls for submission to the will of Allah as revealed to Muhammad. Each tradition, in its own way, offers a vision of how humanity might bridge the chasm between the finite and the infinite.

Yet, in each, there remains an unresolved tension. Either the divine is distant and unknowable, or salvation is earned by human effort, or the self must be dissolved entirely. The great religions often give us noble aspirations but leave us standing at the edge of the ultimate mystery—still longing for a definitive revelation, still searching for a God who comes close enough to touch.

This is where the gospel stands apart. It does not merely point the way—it declares that the Way has come to us. In Christ, the infinite entered the finite. The Creator stepped into creation, not as an idea, not as a vision to a single mystic, but in flesh and blood, witnessed by multitudes, confirmed through history, and vindicated by resurrection. The answers sought in every religion are found not in a system but in a Person.

This is neither to deny the value of other faiths nor to dismiss the sincerity of those who follow them. Indeed, many are closer to truth than they realize. Their moral insights, their reverence for the transcendent, and their longing for justice and peace are not accidents—they are echoes of the original Voice. But echoes, no matter how beautiful, are not the Voice itself.

At this threshold, the question becomes urgent: If all our searching leads to this singular intersection—where human longing meets divine self-revelation—what will we do with it? To see Christ as the fulfillment of all truth claims is to see the arc of history itself bending toward him. Every philosophy, every religion, every human story finds its coherence here.

We now cross from comparative exploration into synthesis. The task ahead is not merely to understand differences but to draw the threads together—to see how reason, morality, science, and faith converge in a single tapestry. The path forward will demand more than belief; it will demand clarity of thought and courage of conviction. We have surveyed the many roads humanity has walked; now we must examine why one road alone can bear the full weight of reality.

This is what I call "The Threshold of Synthesis"—a crossing point. Behind us lies the map of humanity's search for God. Before us lies the question of how all truth, wherever found, must bow to the truth revealed in the life, death, and resurrection of Jesus Christ. We stand ready to step beyond boundaries, into the unifying vision for which all creation has been waiting.

PART 6

Deep Philosophical Synthesis

Chapter 1

The Blindness of Modern Genius

ACROSS HISTORY, THE GREATEST breakthroughs in science were not born from a rejection of God but from a deep belief in him.

Isaac Newton,[1] Johannes Kepler,[2] Galileo Galilei,[3] Robert Boyle,[4] and countless others—these men laid the foundations of modern science while holding a worldview saturated in faith. They saw the universe as the creation of an intelligent, moral, and personal God. They studied the stars, the laws of motion, the mechanics of life, not to dethrone the Creator but to understand his craftsmanship.

Yet today, many modern scientists stand proudly upon their shoulders and deny the very God who gave them the vision to begin their work. They marvel at the equations, the fine-tuning of the cosmos, the breathtaking precision of DNA, and yet refuse to utter the name of the One who tuned, designed, and coded it all.

Consider this: if you walked into a library filled with volumes of perfect prose, would you insist the words arranged themselves?

1. Newton, *Principia*; Force and Popkin, *Books of Nature and Scripture*.
2. Kepler, *Harmonies of the World*, Book V; Caspar, *Kepler*.
3. Galilei, "Letter to the Grand Duchess"; Finocchiaro, *Galileo Affair*.
4. Boyle, *Works of Robert Boyle*; Hunter, *Boyle*.

If you found a piece of software running with flawless logic, would you deny the existence of a programmer? And yet, when the double helix of DNA displays an informational system far more complex than any human code, many scientists will speak of "nature,"[5] "chance,"[6] or "self-organization"[7]—anything but the Coder. This is not merely an intellectual oversight; it is a moral decision.

Acknowledging God as the Designer would mean acknowledging God as the Lawgiver. It would mean admitting that the universe is not a cosmic accident but a moral stage, and that our actions have eternal significance. The denial of God, in this light, is not the triumph of reason but the evasion of responsibility.

The irony is glaring: modern science owes its very existence to a worldview it now seeks to erase. The empirical method was built on the conviction that the universe is ordered because its Creator is orderly. Remove the Creator and you risk unmooring science from the very principles that made it possible.

To claim to see design without a designer is to embrace a contradiction. It is intellectual pride masquerading as objectivity. And as history has shown, pride is the oldest, most destructive blindness of all.

In the chapters ahead, we will not merely argue for God's existence—we will demonstrate that the deepest truths of science, philosophy, morality, and human destiny are inseparably bound to him. Without God, the equation of reality collapses. With him, every mystery finds its place.

---

5. Hawking and Mlodinow, *Grand Design*; Sagan, *Cosmos*.
6. Dawkins, *Blind Watchmaker*; Monod, *Chance and Necessity*.
7. Kauffman, *Origins of Order*; Prigogine, *Order Out of Chaos*.

Chapter 2

The First Truth
Why Every Story Must Begin with God

BEFORE THERE WAS TIME, before there was matter, before there was even the concept of "before," there was God. This is not poetry—it is the unavoidable conclusion of reason when it is pursued to its ultimate foundation.

To begin with anything other than God is to begin with a lie. Philosophers have wrestled with the concept of "nothingness" for millennia, but the human mind cannot truly imagine it. Even in our most abstract thoughts, we are forced to conceive of an empty space, a void—but a void is still something. Nothingness is not an empty canvas; it is the absence of the canvas, the absence of color, the absence of the observer. It is, in truth, a concept beyond our reach—and yet modern science often demands that we accept it as the starting point for everything.

Historically, the greatest minds in science and philosophy knew better. Isaac Newton called the universe "the sensorium of God."[1] Johannes Kepler spoke of "thinking God's thoughts after Him."[2] René Descartes began with "I think, therefore I am"[3]—but

1. Newton, *Principia*, 543.
2. Kepler, *Harmonies of the World*, Book V, 350.
3. Descartes, *Meditations on First Philosophy*, 35–36.

even that was built on his prior acceptance of God as the guarantor of truth and reality. These were not men of blind faith; they were men of piercing intellect, who understood that design without a Designer is not science—it is superstition dressed as reason.

Today, however, much of the scientific world has chosen to begin its story in the middle, skipping over the first chapter entirely. They marvel at the fine-tuning of the universe—the delicate balance of physical constants, the incomprehensible precision of DNA code—and yet refuse to acknowledge the One who tuned it, the Coder who wrote it. If a programmer sees a string of code in a machine, he knows there was a coder. If an archaeologist sees a carved stone, she knows there was an artisan. Why, then, do some scientists see the most intricate code known to man—the DNA blueprint for life—and shrug at the idea of a Mind behind it? It is not logic that drives this; it is selective blindness.

To say "we can explain everything without God" is to confuse mechanism with origin. A physicist may describe gravity, but gravity did not create itself. A biologist may describe the function of DNA, but DNA did not write itself.

The laws of physics cannot legislate themselves into being. Logic demands that if there is law, there is a lawgiver. If there is information, there is an informer. If there is design, there is a designer.

From a purely human standpoint, it is necessary—even inevitable—to begin with God. Remove him from the first line of the story, and the rest of the narrative collapses into contradiction. Start with nothing, and you are left with nothing. Start with God, and you have the foundation upon which every truth, every law, every moral standard can rest.

This is why the Bible begins at Gen 1:1 not with an argument for God's existence but with a declaration: "In the beginning, God." Not "In the beginning, matter." Not "In the beginning, chance."

The beginning belongs to God—and to deny him is to deny the very possibility of a coherent universe.

If we are to seek truth with integrity, we must start where truth itself begins. And the first truth is this: God is.

Chapter 3

The Architecture of Reality

IF THE UNIVERSE WERE truly the product of pure chaos, as some scientists claim,[1] then studying it would be a futile endeavor. Chaos, by definition, is randomness without order—and true randomness would never yield the same result twice. In such a reality, experiments would be meaningless because there would be no repeatable laws or patterns to observe. Yet the very success of science depends on the opposite: the fact that the universe operates according to consistent, repeatable laws and dynamics. Gravity works the same today as it did yesterday; the chemical reactions that sustain life follow the same principles no matter where in the cosmos they occur. This undeniable order is not an incidental feature—it is the foundation that makes all study, measurement, and prediction possible. Order implies structure, and structure points inevitably to a source. Just as a code requires a coder, the laws of the universe require a Lawgiver—an intelligence behind the order that enables our minds to uncover its patterns.

In the beginning, there was not chaos—there was order.

---

1. Hawking and Mlodinow, *Grand Design*, 180; Krauss, *Universe from Nothing*, 170–75; Dawkins, *Blind Watchmaker*, 5; Monod, *Chance and Necessity*, 112.; Prigogine, *Order Out of Chaos*, 10–15; Kauffman, *Origins of Order*, 3–7.

This is not just a poetic claim. It is the unavoidable conclusion of both reason and observation. The deeper we peer into the universe, the more we see mathematical precision and purposeful structure woven into every level of existence. Physics, chemistry, biology, morality—all operate as if the world were built on a vast, interconnected code.

The Physical Order

From the first seconds after the big bang, the constants of physics have been balanced to a degree that defies human comprehension. The gravitational constant, the cosmological constant, the ratio of electrons to protons—each one tuned to within unimaginable tolerances. Alter any of them by even a fraction, and stars could not form, chemistry would not function, life would be impossible.

Scientists call this "fine-tuning,"[2] and yet many refuse to ask the obvious: Who tuned it?

If a single message written in binary code would prove beyond any reasonable doubt that a mind created it, why does the infinitely greater complexity of the cosmos not point even more clearly to an Architect? We accept design in every human-made system—a smartphone, a spacecraft, a work of art—but when faced with the most sophisticated system of all, the human heart hesitates.

The Biological Code

Life itself is built on language—the genetic code. Four chemical "letters" (A, T, C, G) combine into billions of precise sequences in every cell. This is not mere chemistry; it is information. And information, as every scientist and engineer knows, always comes from a mind.

To believe that DNA wrote itself is like believing that a library assembled itself from a hurricane in a paper mill. It is worse,

---

2. Davies, *Goldilocks Enigma*; Rees, *Just Six Numbers*; Barnes, "Fine-Tuning of the Universe."

because the genetic library is self-replicating, self-repairing, and capable of producing not just books but living beings who can think, feel, and love.

The Moral Order

Even beyond physics and biology, there is a moral architecture to reality. Across cultures and history, humans have recognized certain truths: that love is better than hate, justice is better than injustice, courage is better than cowardice. These moral constants are not the result of cultural convenience; they are written into the very fabric of human nature.

To deny them is to deny ourselves.

The Hypocrisy of Selective Recognition

The irony is that scientists are quick to credit design when it suits their field. Archaeologists finding a chipped stone in the desert will declare it evidence of an intelligent craftsman. Cryptographers finding a patterned signal will call it a message. Engineers know that function requires planning.

But when the data points to the greatest Designer of all, the conversation shifts. "It is coincidence." "It is inevitable." "It just happened."[3]

This is not science; this is selective blindness.

The Only Coherent Source

Order—whether mathematical, biological, or moral—demands a source that is both intelligent and powerful enough to establish it. That source must exist before matter, before energy, before time itself. That source must be timeless, immaterial, personal.

That source is God.

---

3. Dawkins, *Blind Watchmaker*, 1; Crick, *What Mad Pursuit*, 138; Shermer, *Why Darwin Matters*, 14–17; Davies, *Goldilocks Enigma*, 3–5.

The architecture of reality is not an accident. It is a cathedral—a vast, cosmic structure built not of stone and glass but of space, time, energy, and life. And like every cathedral, it points beyond itself to the One who designed it.

The question is not whether the universe is ordered. It is whether we will acknowledge the Architect.

Chapter 4

The Unity of Truth
From Many Roads to One

STANDING AT THE CROSSROADS of history, philosophy, and faith, we can now see the contours of the entire journey we have walked so far. The great religions of the world, with all their diversity, have attempted to answer the same fundamental questions: Who are we? Why are we here? What is the meaning of our existence? And what, if anything, awaits us beyond the veil of death?

We have seen how Hinduism's layered cosmology seeks truth in cycles of rebirth, how Buddhism offers liberation by extinguishing desire, how Judaism stands as the ancient covenant between God and a chosen people, and how Islam calls for submission to a singular will. Each, in its own way, has glimpsed fragments of the truth—but no single one offers the complete and definitive revelation humanity needs.

This is not to dismiss their value. The echoes of truth within them are real, but they are precisely that—echoes, not the Voice itself.

They prepare the mind to search for more, but they cannot bring the soul to final rest. Their moral structures, their reverence for something higher, their call to live rightly—these are shadows cast by a greater Light.

When we step beyond comparative religion, we find ourselves entering a broader arena—the realm where reason, morality, science, and revelation must all meet without contradiction. This is where the uniqueness of the gospel becomes unshakable. Unlike other paths, Christianity does not begin with humanity climbing toward God—it begins with God descending to humanity. It is not the story of man finding the divine; it is the story of the divine stepping into human history, witnessed, recorded, and vindicated before a watching world.

The question is no longer whether there is truth in various traditions—it is whether there is a truth that can make sense of them all. And here, science itself becomes a surprising ally. For if the universe were chaos, as some claim, it could not be studied. Chaos by definition is pure randomness, producing no consistent patterns to observe. Yet the universe is governed by fixed laws, repeating dynamics, and mathematical elegance. This alone implies a mind behind the order—a Coder behind the code written into DNA, a Designer behind the finely tuned constants of physics.

If there is order, there is a source of that order. If there is information, there is an Author. And if that Author has revealed himself in history—in a way that unites morality, reason, and the deepest longings of the human heart—then all truth, from every discipline and every culture, must converge on him.

This is why the Christian claim is not arrogance but coherence. It is the only worldview in which the moral lawgiver, the scientific order, the philosophical first cause, and the personal Savior are one and the same. The One who spoke galaxies into existence is the same One who spoke forgiveness over a dying thief. The same hands that shaped the laws of physics were pierced for the redemption of humanity.

We now stand at the edge of synthesis. The map of human belief is behind us. Ahead lies the task of drawing every fragment of truth into a single, unbroken whole. This chapter is not an ending but a hinge—the point where the many roads we have walked now lead to the one road that explains them all.

The Unity of Truth

Truth is not an abstract principle. Truth is a Person. And all truth, wherever found, ultimately bends toward him.

Chapter 5

The Law Written on the Heart
Why Morality Points Beyond Evolution

From the dawn of human history, every tribe, every nation, every civilization—no matter how distant in geography or culture—has shared a sense of morality. We may differ in the details, but certain moral instincts are universal: the idea that murder is wrong, that promises should be kept, that children should be protected, that justice matters. Even when people violate these laws, they almost always feel the need to justify themselves, as if appealing to some invisible standard that exists above them.

If morality were simply a product of evolution—an accidental arrangement of neural wiring that happened to give our ancestors a survival edge—then why should it feel so binding? Why should we care about doing what's right even when it comes at great personal cost? Why should a soldier throw himself on a grenade to save his comrades? Why should a stranger run into a burning building to rescue someone they've never met? Evolutionary theory can explain cooperation in small groups when it benefits the survival of shared genes, but it stumbles when confronted with acts of radical self-sacrifice for those outside one's genetic circle.

Morality is not simply a set of survival strategies dressed up in noble language. It is a law written into the very core of our being—a law that speaks not of expediency but of obligation. It is a voice that says, "You ought." And that "ought" carries a weight far beyond instinct or preference.

The Limits of Evolutionary Morality

Those who argue that morality evolved naturally often point to herd animals, primates, and other social creatures that display cooperation and empathy. Yet these behaviors are selective—they often vanish when survival is threatened or when the cost outweighs the benefit.

Human morality, however, stubbornly resists such calculation. We are capable of laying down our lives for complete strangers, of forgiving enemies, of helping those who cannot repay us.

If morality were purely a byproduct of natural selection, we would expect it to collapse under pressure, revealing its pragmatic roots. But history shows countless examples of people who refused to betray their conscience even when it cost them their lives. From the early Christian martyrs to modern-day believers in oppressive regimes, this moral courage defies evolutionary logic.

The Moral Lawgiver

The universality of morality points us to something greater than human invention—it points to a Moral Lawgiver. Laws imply a lawmaker. And the consistency of moral law across cultures suggests that this Lawmaker stands above humanity, transcending any single society or time period.

This is exactly what the apostle Paul meant when he wrote that the law is "written on their hearts" (Rom 2:15). Our conscience is not a random adaptation; it is a direct imprint of God's nature upon us. It is his way of teaching us, in every culture and generation, the principles of life in his kingdom.

Divine Love as the Standard

If we ask why God's moral law is what it is—why it condemns pride, greed, and cruelty, and why it commands humility, generosity, and mercy—the answer is simple: because God is love (1 John 4:8).

Every command, every moral instruction, flows from his nature. Love is not just an emotion he feels; it is the essence of his being. And because of this, his love for all he has created is consistent, unwavering, and eternal. When he teaches us to love our neighbor, to forgive seventy times seven, to lay down our lives for one another, he is not imposing an arbitrary code. He is shaping us into the kind of beings who can dwell with him forever.

Divine love is the moral standard. It is the goal toward which all moral growth points. God is not merely training us to obey rules—he is teaching us to be like him. And one day, when his work is complete, his people will live in perfect harmony with his nature, experiencing divine love forever.

Why Other Worldviews Fail

Materialism cannot provide a grounding for objective morality. If we are only collections of atoms shaped by blind forces, then morality is reduced to personal or cultural preference. Relativism collapses into contradiction, for the moment someone says, "There is no absolute right or wrong," they inevitably appeal to a moral standard when they cry out against injustice.

Even some religious systems falter when they detach morality from the nature of God. In legalistic systems, morality becomes about external compliance rather than inner transformation. In mystical systems, morality can dissolve into subjective feelings, with no stable anchor. Only in the gospel does morality have both a fixed foundation (God's unchanging nature) and a final purpose (our transformation into his likeness).

The Law and Our Destiny

The moral law is not a chain meant to restrict our freedom—it is the path to our true freedom. It is God's way of preparing us for life in his kingdom, where love reigns and selfishness has no place. Just as a musician must learn the laws of harmony before they can improvise beautifully, we must learn the laws of divine love before we can live fully in God's presence.

And this is where morality's connection to eternity becomes clear. If heaven is the realm where God's nature is perfectly expressed, then heaven is the realm of perfect love. The moral training we undergo in this life is preparation for that reality. Every act of forgiveness, every choice to put others before ourselves, every sacrifice made for the sake of truth and goodness—these are steps toward our eternal destiny.

Morality, then, is not the product of evolution. It is the handwriting of God on the human heart. It points us beyond ourselves, beyond survival, to the One who is love itself. And if we follow its call, it will lead us home.

Chapter 6

The Mystery of Consciousness

THE SOUL'S UNYIELDING LIGHT opening the mystery of consciousness isn't just a scientific puzzle—it's our most undeniable experience. Technology, computation, reductionist theories—they may describe brain activity, but none capture the vividness of being "you" right now. Philosopher David Chalmers calls this the "hard problem"[1]—the gap between physical brain processes and lived experience, which modern science has yet to bridge.

A Double Paradox

On the one hand, the universe exhibits remarkable order—its mathematical laws, physical constants, and predictability allow science to exist at all. Physicist Eugene Wigner famously called this "the unreasonable effectiveness of mathematics"[2]—a kind of awe-inspiring gift we use without fully understanding why it works. But here's the deeper puzzle: not only is the universe intelligible, but our minds are built to understand it. Why should random particles give rise to beings capable of decoding cosmic harmony?

---

1. Chalmers, *Conscious Mind*, 3–5.
2. Wigner, "Unreasonable Effectiveness of Mathematics."

Consciousness Theories and the Evidence

One of the most promising models is Integrated Information Theory (IIT), proposed by Giulio Tononi. IIT asserts that consciousness corresponds to a system's ability to integrate information in a unified way—measured by a quantity called Φ (*phi*).[3] In humans, our brains exhibit high levels of integrated information, which explains why simple systems—like a calculator or isolated neurons—aren't conscious.

The theory even extends into clinical practice: measures like the perturbational complexity index (PCI), grounded in IIT, help assess whether unresponsive patients remain conscious.[4] Still, challenges remain—IIT faces critiques around its philosophical assumptions and empirical testability. But even within its critics, there's recognition that consciousness demands more than neural function; it demands integration that points beyond the physical.

Why This Points Beyond Materialism

Materialism—reducing consciousness to chemicals and electrical signals—can't explain why subjective experience exists at all. If our minds are chemically determined, why should they reflect truth? Why can we experience, choose, reason, love? Logically, a purely physical origin can't ground such phenomena in reality, much less harness them to grasp universal order.

Anchoring Mind in Divine Origin

Christianity offers profound coherence: we are conscious because we bear God's image—endowed with the capacity to know, love, and choose. An ordered universe and ordered minds both make sense if there is an intelligent, rational Creator who made us with

---

3. Tononi, "Consciousness as Integrated Information"; Tononi, "Information Integration Theory of Consciousness"; Tononi and Koch, "Consciousness."

4. Casali et al., "Theoretically Based Index"; Sarasso et al., "Consciousness and Complexity."

intention. Consciousness is a spark of the divine *Logos* (the ultimate rational Lawgiver).

A final, urgent exhortation to deny God's reality while living as conscious, moral agents is like denying the sun on the brightest day. Consciousness isn't merely property of the mind—it's its calling. It beckons us to seek truth, to press beyond material shadows, and to recognize the Mind that made it all.

Chapter 7

The Universal Law
Why Morality Cannot Be Erased

It does not matter whether a society exists in the bronze age, the space age, or in some imagined future on the surface of Mars—without a shared moral framework, civilization collapses. This is not speculation; it is history's verdict. Every enduring society has carried, in one form or another, a code of right and wrong that transcended the whims of its leaders. Without it, law becomes nothing more than the preferences of the powerful, and the powerless are devoured.

The modern mind often assumes that science will eventually replace moral law. After all, science can describe why the planets move, how the brain processes information, or what DNA looks like under a microscope. But science, for all its wonders, has no power to answer the question: What ought we to do?

If morality were truly optional—if all that existed were atoms and forces—then there is no reason theft should be illegal, no reason murder should be punished, no reason promises should be kept. If you steal on Mars, why should it be wrong? If you kill in deep space, who will say it is evil? In a purely scientific universe without God, these concepts dissolve. They are reduced to social conventions that can be discarded the moment they become inconvenient.

And yet, even the most secular societies cannot escape moral law. We see this in the very structure of our legal systems. We punish theft because we believe that life and property have inherent worth. We protect the vulnerable because we believe the strong do not have the right to exploit the weak. These convictions are not born from chemistry or physics—they are the imprint of God's moral order on the human soul.

If humanity ever spreads beyond Earth, the first thing we will carry with us—before any technology, before any architecture—will be our moral code. Without it, the colonies will tear themselves apart. This truth is not dependent on religion as a social construct; it is dependent on the reality that morality comes from a Lawgiver who stands above all cultures, planets, and eras.

Even the most brilliant scientists, standing on the pinnacle of human achievement, remain bound by this reality. They can split the atom but cannot split good from evil. They can send a spacecraft beyond the solar system but cannot send morality into exile. That fact alone should humble them—for it shows that they still answer to Someone higher than themselves.

If science were the final authority, then law would have no binding force except consensus. But consensus changes; truth does not. A moral law rooted in God's nature is not subject to human vote. It is the same yesterday, today, and forever. And wherever humanity travels—to the edges of the galaxy or into the deepest reaches of the mind—we will find that this law has arrived before us.

Chapter 8

The Map We Abandoned

FOR AS LONG AS humanity has walked the earth, we have been on a voyage. The waters have been unpredictable—sometimes calm and glistening, sometimes violent and unforgiving—but we have never been without a map. This map, the moral law revealed by God and recorded in Scripture, has guided kings and shepherds alike. It has steered empires through storms, corrected wandering nations, and shown individuals the way back when they drifted too far.

Every culture that has flourished for generations had, at its foundation, a moral compass aligned with the truths of this map. Whether they knew it or not, their laws echoed its commands, their values borrowed from its wisdom, and their vision of justice mirrored the One who authored it. The shore—the eternal home for which we were made—remained visible on the horizon because the map kept us on course.

But today, something remarkable and tragic has happened. We have thrown the map overboard. Not because it failed—but because we, in our arrogance, decided we no longer needed it. Like sailors who have survived storms thanks to its accuracy, we now claim the storms were never that bad, and the map was never that important. We insist we can chart our own course with new tools—philosophies built on sand, morality rewritten to suit personal preference, and scientific achievements mistaken for moral authority.

The results are already visible. The further we drift from the shore, the more featureless and endless the ocean becomes. We are surrounded by waves but cannot tell which way is forward. We have traded certainty for disorientation, truth for opinion, and eternal anchors for passing trends.

This is not merely a cultural crisis—it is a spiritual one. Because the truth is this: you cannot sail without a map and expect to find your destination. Without God's moral law, there is no fixed north. Without the gospel, there is no hope when storms close in. Without the eternal shore in sight, we will wander until exhaustion takes us.

History bears witness to this reality. Civilizations that honored God's principles—even imperfectly—built lasting institutions, created art that lifted the soul, and established laws that protected the vulnerable. Civilizations that scorned the moral map eventually collapsed under the weight of their own corruption. The map was never the problem. It was our willingness to follow it that determined survival or ruin.

And here lies the greatest irony: the very societies now convinced they can sail without God are still benefiting from the stability his map created. Modern laws against murder, theft, and injustice are echoes of commandments given thousands of years ago. The human rights we defend as "universal" exist only because the map declared that all people are made in the image of God. Our freedoms did not appear out of the ocean mist—they came from the shore we are now abandoning.

Refusing to acknowledge this is like claiming you can navigate the sea without ever looking at the stars, while still relying on the positions the stars have fixed for centuries. It is self-deception at its finest.

And the danger is not just theoretical. A ship that drifts too far loses not only sight of the shore but also the knowledge of how to return. A generation that grows up without the map will not even know it existed. They will inherit an ocean without direction, a voyage without meaning, and a life without hope.

This is why the gospel is not just a private belief—it is the essential chart for the human race. It is the only map that leads to safe harbor because it comes from the One who made both the ocean and the shore. And when humanity finally admits it is lost, when the waves become too high and the horizon too dark, that map will still be waiting, unchanged, ready to guide us home.

The question is whether we will humble ourselves to pick it up again before it is too late. Yet, to abandon the map is not simply to lose a set of traditions or to drift into harmless uncertainty—it is to sever ourselves from the very coordinates that make civilization possible. A moral axis is not a cultural ornament; it is the foundation of law, justice, and human dignity. Without it, our reasoning becomes unmoored, our science loses its moral compass, and even the most advanced societies begin to collapse inward under the weight of their own contradictions.

History shows that every enduring civilization—whether consciously or not—has operated according to fixed moral principles. These principles are not the product of human invention alone; they are reflections of something higher, an unchanging source from which meaning flows. The map we inherited is not the random sketch of our ancestors—it is the charting of a reality grounded in the character of God himself. It is not merely that God drew the map; in Christ, he became the Map, the Way, the Truth, and the Life. Without this anchor, science risks becoming a tool without purpose, power without wisdom. Human rights, detached from their divine source, become negotiable, subject to the shifting will of the majority or the decree of the powerful. The moral order, like gravity, does not need our belief to operate—but our survival depends on recognizing and aligning ourselves with it. As we move forward into the next stage of this journey, the question is no longer whether humanity can navigate without the map—we already see the consequences of trying. The question is whether we will have the humility to return to it, to let the One who made us lead us back to the safe shores we have drifted from. This is the threshold where moral history meets divine revelation, and where the search for truth must inevitably confront the Source of truth.

Chapter 9

Guardrails Against the Abyss

CIVILIZATIONS DO NOT COLLAPSE overnight. They drift. The fall of a nation, like the fall of a man, begins with the quiet removal of boundaries. A principle ignored here, a tradition dismissed there, and soon the guardrails that once kept us from plunging into darkness are rusted through or stripped away entirely.

Some see morality as a cage—an outdated system of rules meant to limit freedom. But morality, rightly understood, is not a cage; it is a railing at the edge of a cliff. It is the structure that keeps us from tumbling into chaos.

Science can measure the drop. Philosophy can debate the meaning of the fall. But only a moral law—and a moral Lawgiver—can keep us from stepping over the edge. Without these guardrails, even the most advanced society can become little more than a technologically sophisticated jungle, where the strong dominate the weak and truth is whatever the powerful decide.

History shows it again and again: when morality is untethered from a transcendent source, cultures begin to bend reality to suit their desires. Laws that once reflected eternal truths become tools of convenience. Justice becomes selective. Freedom becomes license. And license, inevitably, becomes bondage.

The paradox is this: true freedom exists only within limits. A ship can roam the sea because it respects the hull that keeps it afloat. A bridge can carry us forward because it refuses to abandon its structure. And a civilization can prosper only when its people accept that some truths are fixed—unchangeable, regardless of the times.

The moral law is not an invention of man; it is a reflection of God's nature. Remove God and you remove the authority that gives the law its force. Remove the law, and you remove the framework that gives civilization its stability. What remains is the abyss.

These are the guardrails: truth that does not shift with opinion, justice that does not bow to popularity, love that does not demand self-erasure. Without them, progress becomes directionless, and power becomes god.

We must decide, here and now, whether to keep the rails in place—not because we fear the darkness but because we love the light. For if we lose them, the fall will not be sudden, but it will be certain. And in that long descent, even the brightest achievements of humanity will flicker and fade, swallowed by the abyss they refused to acknowledge.

Chapter 10

The Final Proof
When All Roads Lead to God

WE HAVE STOOD IN temples, synagogues, mosques, and monasteries. We have crossed the terrain of scientific theories and philosophical thought experiments. We have examined the moral laws that govern human societies and the moral collapses that happen when they are abandoned. We have sifted through history's testimony and the heart's deepest intuitions. Now the paths converge.

The human search for truth is not a random scattering of guesses; it is the echo of a single Voice that calls through every culture and every age. The hunger for meaning, the longing for justice, the instinct to worship, the recognition of beauty, the ache for redemption—all of these are fingerprints of the same Author. We have seen this in the structure of the cosmos, where chaos could never produce the order we can study. We have seen it in morality, where the law is written on human hearts before it is ever written in human codes. We have seen it in the testimony of witnesses who walked with Jesus, ate with him after the resurrection, and gave their lives to testify to what they had seen.

At every fork in the road, the evidence points in one direction. Hinduism hints at divine immanence but leaves salvation to countless cycles of self-effort. Buddhism understands the poison of pride but fades the self into nothingness instead of redeeming it. Judaism cherishes the covenant but still waits for the fulfillment already come. Islam affirms one God but offers no proof beyond the word of one man in one cave. The modern secular worldview prizes reason but saws off the branch it sits on by denying the Source of reason itself.

The gospel alone unites every thread—the Creator entering creation, not as an abstract idea but as a Person who could be touched, questioned, and crucified.

A God who is not content to be guessed at, but who speaks, acts, and proves his love by paying the debt himself. A truth that withstands history's scrutiny, answers philosophy's questions, and fulfills the moral law while offering mercy to lawbreakers.

Here, the evidence is not merely cumulative—it is convergent. When independent lines of inquiry all point to the same conclusion, the weight of proof becomes undeniable. And the conclusion is this: every honest search for truth will, if followed to its end, lead to the foot of the cross.

But this chapter is not simply an intellectual checkpoint. It is a mirror. You, the reader, have walked these roads with me. You have tested claims, weighed evidence, and traced meaning through the corridors of history and the laboratory of the mind. And now, as with every pilgrim who has come this far, you stand at the same threshold: What will you do with this Christ?

The final proof is not in the arguments alone. It is in the encounter. Reason has done its work—it has cleared the fog, lit the path, and shown the destination. But it cannot walk the last few steps for you. That choice—that step—is yours.

We close part 6 with the inescapable truth: there is no road that leads away from God, only roads that lead toward him, some longer and more winding than others. History, science, morality, and the deepest longings of the human soul all testify together. The map we abandoned, the laws we ignored, the truths we doubted—they have all led us back here.

Part 7 will ask what it means to live in light of this reality, to stand not only as one who has found the truth but as one entrusted to carry it into a world still searching. We will see how faith, reason, and history are not relics of the past but tools for the future—a future shaped by the God who has made himself known.

PART 7

The Great Convergence

Chapter 1

Where All Truths Meet

HISTORY IS OFTEN TOLD as the story of human ambition, empires rising and falling, discoveries and revolutions shaping our world. But what if the truest history is the one heaven itself has been watching—a story that began not with humanity but with a rebellion among divine beings?

Before humanity walked the earth, Scripture tells us there was war in heaven (Rev 12). Created in glory, some of the highest angels turned from God, seeking their own throne. This rebellion did not happen in a place of ignorance or weakness but in the perfection of God's presence. If sin could be born even there, the question for all creation became urgent: Who is worthy to rule, and what is the nature of true greatness?

God's answer was unexpected. He created a new kind of being—not from the radiant substance of heaven but from the dust of the ground. Fragile. Mortal. Bound to a physical world. And yet, into that dust he breathed his own life (Gen 2:7). It was a deliberate choice: to create the lowest in order to raise them to the highest. The arc was set—from dust to divine.

Psalm 8:5 captures the paradox: "You have made them a little lower than the angels, yet crowned them with glory and honor." Paul would later declare in 1 Cor 6:3 that the redeemed will "judge angels." The last would become first, not by their own strength but by learning to choose God's love over every competing voice.

Why does this matter for our place in the timeline of history?

Because the whole human story—from the garden to the cross, from resurrection to the promised restoration—is the demonstration of God's power to take the lowly and exalt them. In Christ, God himself entered into dust, took on flesh, and walked among us—showing that divine love is not simply above creation but willing to dwell within it.

Through Israel, God laid the prophetic groundwork. Through the incarnation, he brought the answer into the world. Through the resurrection, he revealed that death—the last weapon of pride—had been broken. And through the church, he continues the transformation, calling people from every tribe and tongue, not just to be saved from sin but to be prepared for glory.

When we stand at the end of history, the angels themselves will see the justice of God's plan. The proud fell from glory into ruin; the humble rose from dust into eternal splendor. This is the great reversal, the cosmic vindication of God's love and wisdom.

The timeline is no accident. From rebellion in heaven, to the creation of mankind, to the cross and resurrection, and finally to the renewal of all things—each event is a thread in one tapestry, revealing that all of history bends toward one truth: that God's holiness and love are the foundation on which all creation must stand.

This is the great convergence—not just of faith and reason but of heaven and earth, of the first creation and the new. It is the story that makes sense of every other story. And at its heart is the mystery that dust, touched by divine love, can become more glorious than the brightest star.

The question is no longer whether the plan is unfolding. The question is whether we will take our place in it.

Chapter 2

The Timeline That Was Never Chance

History is not a series of disconnected events strung together by coincidence. It is a tapestry—and when you step back far enough, the pattern becomes impossible to ignore. For those willing to examine it honestly, the flow of history reveals a precision that no random process could ever replicate. Every empire's rise and fall, every cultural shift, and every pivotal breakthrough moves us toward a singular point: the life, death, and resurrection of Jesus Christ, and the gospel that followed.

From the dawn of human civilization, God has worked through both the faithful and the faithless to prepare the stage. The Roman Empire's infrastructure—its roads, common language, and political unity—became the perfect vehicle for the rapid spread of Christianity. Centuries earlier, the Babylonian exile refined Israel's identity and preserved the Scriptures in a way that would later testify to Christ's fulfillment of prophecy. Even the Greek philosophical tradition, though unaware of the coming Messiah, provided the intellectual framework for early Christians to articulate the truth to the wider world.

The prophecies were not vague hopes but precise declarations. The Messiah's birthplace, the manner of his death, the timing of his ministry—all foretold centuries before and fulfilled exactly. This is not the mark of chance. This is the signature of a Mind that governs both the grand and the granular details of history.

Skeptics might call it selective hindsight, but this pattern is not a trick of perception—it is confirmed by the sheer weight of converging evidence. Multiple independent historical threads align in ways no human planner could orchestrate over millennia. If this were mere coincidence, the probability would be so astronomically small as to be indistinguishable from zero.

But the convergence does not stop at the ancient world. The same precision has continued through the centuries: the preservation of Scripture despite persecution, the endurance of the gospel through the fall of empires, the translation of the Bible into every major language, and the way global communication now carries the name of Jesus to places previously unreachable.

These turning points were not accidents. They were appointments. God's plan has unfolded with a balance of sovereignty and human freedom, guiding history toward the ultimate reconciliation of all creation.

This is why the story of the world is not just about kings, wars, or discoveries. It is about a God who stepped into his own creation at the exact moment when the world was most prepared to see him—and who continues to guide history toward its final, promised conclusion.

When we see this, the great convergence becomes undeniable: history, prophecy, science, and morality are not separate paths but tributaries of one great river, flowing inevitably toward the truth of the gospel. And if history itself has been this purposeful, then so is your life within it.

Chapter 3

When Every Pursuit Leads to God

The Necessity of Meaning

Without the perfect God of the gospel, there is no meaning—only illusions. Any alternative is, by definition, incomplete because no one and nothing outside of God can supply a meaning that is both eternal and morally perfect. Without him, every pursuit—whether laws, work, family, morality, or art—becomes a temporary construction without a foundation.

People often say, "I don't know the purpose of life," as if ignorance somehow excuses apathy. But that uncertainty is not a destination—it is a summons. Not knowing yet is a vastly different thing from there being no answer at all. The truth exists, and it is your duty to seek it. Your lack of awareness does not erase reality any more than closing your eyes erases the sun.

If the answer were not God, then all moral systems, all meaning, would collapse instantly, because their very coherence depends on an unchanging source. The fact that they remain—however imperfectly—proves that something is holding them in place. That "something" is not an abstract concept or a blind force. It is a Mind. It is a Person. It is God.

Without him, we are robots in a self-perpetuating system, responding to programming we cannot explain and serving purposes we cannot define. But with him, we are participants in a story of love, justice, and truth that not only explains why we exist—it calls us to rise and live worthy of that purpose.

Chapter 4

The Timeline Revealed

HISTORY IS NOT A random scatter of events. Step back far enough and a pattern emerges—too coherent to be coincidence, too interlocked to be accidental. Follow four long threads through time—(1) key world events and empires, (2) scientific breakthroughs, (3) moral revolutions, and (4) fulfilled prophecies—and you find that they converge on, and then flow outward from, the life, death, and resurrection of Jesus Christ. What follows is a clear, era-by-era sweep that makes the arc visible.

Ancient Foundations: From Promise to Preparation

- Abraham to Israel: A people is called not because of power but promise—a through-line of blessing "to all nations." A moral monotheism emerges in a pagan world, anchoring justice to the character of God rather than to kings or caprice.
- The Prophets: Hope is sharpened into expectation—of a Messiah, of a suffering servant, of a new covenant. Specific markers appear: Bethlehem for the ruler's birth (Mic 5:2), a servant pierced and despised yet bringing healing (Isa 53), a king entering Jerusalem humbly on a donkey (Zech 9:9), a

righteous one not abandoned to decay (Ps 16:10), hands and feet wounded with enemies casting lots (Ps 22).

- The Exile and Return: Israel's Scriptures are collated, copied, and translated (e.g., the Septuagint), spreading the vocabulary of covenant, sin, sacrifice, and hope across the Mediterranean—concepts that will make the gospel instantly intelligible beyond Judea.

The Roman Hinge: Roads, Language, and the Fullness of Time

- Pax Romana: An empire knits provinces together with roads, sea lanes, and a common legal framework. Greek remains the lingua franca; ideas can travel.
- The "Fullness of Time": Into this precise window, Jesus is born, teaches, is crucified, and is raised. His followers proclaim a public message—witnessed events, not private visions—across a network uniquely suited for rapid spread.
- Prophecy Meets History: Within a generation, as Jesus foretold, the temple is destroyed (AD 70), ending the sacrificial system and fixing the meaning of his once-for-all sacrifice. Daniel's timeline anticipates an "anointed one" cut off before the city and sanctuary fall; history meets the marker.[1]

Outward Flow: From a Marginal Sect to a Global Axis

- Early Church: Persecution purifies and does not extinguish it. Letters and Gospels circulate; eyewitnesses die rather than deny. The moral vision—mercy for enemies, dignity for the poor, chastity, truth-telling—creates a counterculture that slowly reshapes the empire.

---

1. Dan 9:25–26.

The Timeline Revealed

- Collapse and Continuity: Rome falls, but the gospel does not. Monasteries preserve texts; cathedrals embody a universe of order and meaning in stone; hospitals and universities emerge from Christian visions of charity and truth.
- Translation and Transmission: Scripture moves into the vernacular. Printing multiplies Bibles. Literacy spreads because the word matters for every person, not merely elites.

Scientific Breakthroughs: An Ordered Cosmos, a Knowable Mind

- The Assumption Behind Science: Laws of nature are stable and intelligible—because reality is authored by a rational Mind. This conviction births sustained experimental science in a civilization saturated with the idea of creation and providence.
- Key Milestones (a sweep, not a catalogue): Copernicus and Kepler map the heavens; Newton formulates universal gravitation; Maxwell unifies electricity and magnetism; the "beginning" implied by modern cosmology replaces the ancient assumption of an eternal universe; the cosmic background radiation confirms a universe that began; DNA reveals information and code at the heart of life.
- The Convergence: Each advance relies on order, mathematics, and repeatability. Science explains many mechanisms, but the very possibility of explanation assumes a cosmos that is not chaos. That assumption coheres naturally with "In the beginning God created" (Gen 1:1)—and with the *Logos* who upholds all things.

Moral Revolutions: The Image of God in Public Life

- Human Dignity: The radical claim that every human bears God's image fuels movements that remake law and conscience—care for the sick, elevation of the poor, the intrinsic worth of women and children.

- Abolition and Reform: From the abolition of the slave trade and slavery in the modern era to campaigns against child labor and for universal education, the moral grammar is explicitly Christian: persons are not property; the strong owe the weak; justice must be rooted in truth, not utility.
- Civil Rights and Nonviolence: Appeals to the Sermon on the Mount and *Imago Dei* carry moral revolutions forward. Even critics of Christianity borrow its ethical capital when they speak of rights that cannot be revoked by the state.[2]

Fulfilled Prophecies and Historical Markers

- Specific Messianic Signs: Birth in Bethlehem (Mic 5:2); a suffering, pierced servant (Isa 53); entry into Jerusalem on a donkey (Zech 9:9); lots cast for garments and pierced hands/feet (Ps 22); the Holy One not seeing decay (Ps 16:10)—these are not vague generalities but recognizable contours that line up with the Gospel narratives.
- Jesus' Predictions: The fall of Jerusalem and the Temple within that generation (Luke 21; Mark 13) occurs in AD 70, ending sacrifices and underlining the once-for-all nature of the cross.
- Israel Among the Nations: Scattered, preserved, and—after long centuries—regathered as a modern state, a development many readers have associated with prophetic trajectories.[3] Whatever one's eschatology, the persistence of Israel through dispersal is historically singular and biblically resonant.

2. Holland, *Dominion*; Nietzsche, *On the Genealogy of Morals*; MacIntyre, *After Virtue*, 51–61; Habermas, *Awareness of What Is Missing*.

3. Kaiser, *Messiah in the Old Testament*, 218–30; Rydelnik, *Messianic Hope*, 213–25; McDermott, Understanding the Jewish Roots, 312–30; Blaising and Block, *Dispensationalism, Israel and the Church*, 157–80; Aharoni and Avi-Yonah, "Introduction," in *Macmillan Bible Atlas*.

The Timeline Revealed

The patterns you can't unsee put the threads together. Empires rise and provide roads, languages, and law at precisely the moment needed for a public, testable gospel to go global. Scriptures and expectations are prepared in advance. Scientific inquiry flourishes on assumptions that mirror a created, ordered cosmos. Moral revolutions lean on the Christian claim that every person bears God's image. Prophecies align with events that anchor the gospel in history.

This is not a collage of lucky breaks; it is a symphony. Independent themes—history, science, morality, prophecy—resolve into one melody when heard together. The convergence point is Christ. And from that point, the streams flow outward again—renewing persons, families, institutions, and nations wherever the gospel is taken seriously.

Dust to Divine—The Meaning of the Arc

Because the plan reaches higher than rescue. It is not only that God saves; it is that he elevates. From dust he breathes life; from weakness he brings glory. The rebellion of pride is answered not by raw force but by a demonstration: beings of earth, freely choosing love, are raised above the angels in Christ. History's timeline is the classroom of the universe, where heaven learns what pride denied—that God's love is wiser, stronger, and more beautiful than any throne seized by force.

If this arc is real, rejecting it is not neutrality; it is blindness. The roads of world events, science, moral awakening, and prophecy do not meander into meaninglessness. They lead to a cross on a hill and an empty tomb—and from there into a kingdom where truth and love are one.

Chapter 5

Justice

The Moral Compass of the Universe

Justice is not a synonym for "morality in general." It is morality made public—truth, duty, and mercy translated into laws, judgments, and repair. This chapter doesn't re-argue meaning; it shows why the world you can touch (courts, rights, protection of the weak) collapses without God.

What Justice Is (and Is Not)

Justice is the right ordering of communal life. It includes retributive justice (wrong answered), distributive justice (goods owed), and restorative justice (harm repaired). Where justice is present, truth is told, promises are kept, the weak are protected, the strong are restrained, and the community is healed.

Why Secular Foundations Fail

- *Utilitarianism*—If outcomes alone rule, injustice to the few becomes a feature, not a bug.

- *Social Contract*—If justice is invented, it can be reinvented by the strong.

- *Evolutionary Accounts*—Cooperation is strategy, not obligation; rights evaporate when inconvenient. Each account makes justice contingent. But a contingent justice cannot bind consciences across times and cultures.

Answering Euthyphro

Is something just because God commands it, or does he command it because it is just?[1]

The Gospel's answer: God commands the just because he is Justice.

Law flows from nature; the moral law is reality's moral shape, derived from God's unchanging character.

Justice is neither above God nor beneath him; it is in him.

Equal Dignity and the Imago Dei: Only the image of God grounds equal worth for every person—regardless of power, usefulness, or tribe. This dethrones castes and denies every hierarchy that treats people as things. It explains why slaves cannot be property, the poor cannot be disposable, the unborn cannot be voiceless, the elderly cannot be set aside, and enemies cannot be dehumanized.

History: When the Map Was Open (One Lens, Not a Recap)

Where the gospel was taken seriously, public justice measurably advanced—imperfectly, but undeniably: abolition of the slave trade and slavery, reforms in labor and child welfare, education and hospitals for the least, and nonviolent movements rooted in the Sermon on the Mount. Even the most secular arguments for

---

1. Plato, *Euthyphro*, 10a, in *Five Dialogues*.

human rights borrow this moral grammar—rights presume a Right-Giver.

When justice becomes vengeance detached from God, justice curdles into retribution without redemption—accusation without absolution, courts of public opinion without due process, moral zeal with no path to forgiveness. It punishes but cannot heal.

Where justice and mercy meet at the cross, justice is not relaxed; it is fulfilled. The debt is not ignored; it is paid. Mercy is not sentiment; it is reconciliation. Only here do justice and mercy embrace without remainder: the Lawgiver bears the law's penalty so the lawbreaker can be made new.

Guardrails for a Just Society (Actionable, Public, Testable)

- *Truthfulness*—Laws conform to reality; propaganda is excluded.
- *Equality Before the Law*—No privilege for the powerful or popular.
- *Protection of the Weak*—Justice is measured by the fate of the least.
- *Proportionality and Due Process*—Power is checked; punishment fits the crime.
- *Restoration*—Repentance, forgiveness, and repair are possible.

Horizon and Hope

If there is no God, ultimate justice is impossible; many evils go unanswered. If the Judge lives, no deed is lost and no wound unseen. Final judgment is the guarantee that freedom will not be devoured by cruelty forever—and, in Christ, judgment becomes vindication and renewal.

Dust to Divine Justice (The Unique Thread)

God's answer to primordial pride was not annihilation but elevation: to raise a people from dust who freely learn to love what he loves. Practicing justice is training for glory—it is the public rehearsal of heaven's harmony.

The Decision

If justice is real, it must rest on more than opinion, fashion, or force. It rests on God—and it is secured at the cross. Begin where justice and mercy meet; then rise to build what you now know to be true.

Chapter 6

Knowledge and Beauty
When Truth and Wonder Point Beyond Matter

WE HAVE TRACED MEANING, justice, and history to their source. Two great rivers remain to complete the convergence: knowledge and beauty. One answers the mind's hunger for truth, the other the soul's ache for wonder. If either can be fully explained by matter alone, then the gospel is one story among many. But if both ultimately transcend matter, then they, too, bend toward the same horizon: God.

1. *What Is Knowledge?* Knowledge is not bare data; it is true belief with warrant. It requires not only perception but trustworthy faculties, not only reasons but reasons that connect with reality. When you say "I know," you are claiming more than a useful habit; you are claiming contact with what is. The question is, why should human minds, born of dust, be reliably aimed at truth?

2. *The Reliability Problem for Materialism*—If materialism is true—if minds are nothing but neurochemical machines shaped solely by survival—then truth is incidental. Evolution selects for behaviors that help an organism reproduce, not for beliefs that happen to be true. A false belief can be just

Knowledge and Beauty

as adaptive as a true one, so long as the behavior it produces aids survival. On that account, the probability that our cognition is generally reliable is low or inscrutable. But if we have no good reason to trust our cognitive faculties, then we have no good reason to trust the belief in materialism either. A worldview that undercuts the reliability of reason saws off the branch on which it sits.

3. *The Christian Account: Mind from Mind*—Christianity reverses the burden. Reason is reliable because it is derivative, not accidental. A rational Creator made a rational cosmos and rational creatures within it. The *Logos*—divine reason—authors the world with order and invites minds made in his image to discover that order. On this account, knowledge is not a cosmic accident but a vocation. To know is to think God's thoughts after him, within the limits of creaturely finitude.

4. *Mathematics*—The language no one invented: abstract symbols scribbled in human minds, maps so precisely onto the structure of reality. We did not coerce the universe into obeying calculus or group theory; we discovered a grammar already there. Elegance, symmetry, and inevitability mark the greatest mathematical insights; they feel found, not manufactured. If numbers and laws are merely human conventions, nature's obedience to them is a miracle without a cause. If the cosmos is authored, their fit is expected: truth in the mind of God reflected in the patterns of creation.

5. *Beauty*—More than taste, beauty is often dismissed as subjective. Yet, we recognize traits of beauty that recur across eras and cultures: unity with variety, proportion, harmony, clarity, depth. We call certain proofs "beautiful,"[1] certain theories "elegant,"[2] certain pieces of music "sublime."[3] The same features appear in the spiral of a shell, the architecture of a

1. Hardy, *Mathematician's Apology*.
2. Weinberg, *Dreams of a Final Theory*; Dirac, *Directions in Physics*.
3. Burke, *Philosophical Enquiry*.

cathedral, the structure of a symphony, and the equations of physics. If beauty were nothing but private preference, its cross-cultural convergence would be inexplicable. Beauty behaves like a property of reality—one that awakens joy when encountered by a rightly tuned soul.

6. *Beauty: The Summons of Wonder*—The tug of the sublime beauty does more than please; it summons. A night sky thick with stars, a violin line that seems to lean into eternity, a landscape that hushes the heart—these moments feel like communications, as if reality itself were saying, "There is more." Material explanations can catalog neural firings; they cannot account for why wonder carries the signature of meaning. We do not merely react; we sense that beauty points beyond itself, as a window admits light from a world outside the room.

7. *Truth, Goodness, Beauty: The Lost Triad*—The older wisdom named these three the "transcendentals"—properties of being itself. They belong together: truth without goodness becomes cruelty; goodness without truth becomes sentiment; beauty without either becomes manipulation. Modernity split them apart; the gospel reunites them in a single Life. In Christ, truth is personal (he is the Truth), goodness is self-giving (he lays down his life), and beauty is cruciform (splendor through sacrifice). The cross is not the denial of beauty but its purification: glory that refuses to lie.

8. *Art, Science, and Worship*—When a scientist follows evidence wherever it leads, when a composer serves the inner logic of a melody rather than ego, when an artist renders the world faithfully—each is practicing a kind of obedience. Creativity, at its best, is consecrated curiosity. It honors the world as gift and law at once—given to us to cultivate, governed by structures we did not create. This posture is worship by another name. It is how farmers, coders, parents, teachers, carpenters, and poets—all—become priests of the ordinary, offering their craft back to the Giver in gratitude and truthfulness.

9. *The Ethics of Knowledge and Beauty*—If truth and beauty are real, then they impose obligations. Truth requires honesty, humility, and courage; we must correct ourselves when we are wrong. Beauty requires chastity of the senses; we must refuse to exploit the appetite for wonder. A culture that treats facts as weapons and beauty as bait will lose both—and then lose its soul. A culture that receives truth as gift and beauty as blessing will protect the vulnerable, restrain power with principle, and create works that endure.

10. *The Personal Edge*—You do not pursue knowledge merely to win arguments; you pursue it to live in reality. You do not seek beauty merely to feel; you seek it to become whole. If you refuse their Source, both pursuits will fragment. Knowledge will harden into cynicism, beauty into addiction. If you embrace their Source, both pursuits become sacraments—means by which grace ripens intellect and affection into wisdom and love.

11. *Four Roads, One Destination*—The convergence completed meaning, justice, knowledge, and beauty. Each road, when traveled honestly, reaches the same threshold: our minds and our longings were made for Someone. The world is intelligible because it is spoken. The world is beautiful because it is loved. And we are most ourselves when we answer the Speaker and the Lover with the obedience of faith.

The Unavoidable Decision

You now know enough to choose. It is not honest to say "I do not know if there is meaning" when meaning has been shown, or "I do not know if justice is real" when your conscience testifies, or "I cannot tell if beauty is anything more than taste" when wonder breaks your defenses, or "I cannot trust reason" while using reason to deny its source. The question is not whether the convergence is persuasive. It is whether you will live in the light it provides.

Chapter 7

The Last Turn Before Home

ALL THE ROADS ARE here now. The rivers we followed—meaning, justice, knowledge, beauty; the testimony of history; the order of the cosmos; the whisper of conscience—have converged into a single current. This is not an archive of arguments. It is a shoreline. We began with questions. We end with sight. The world is intelligible because it is spoken. The human person is precious because he bears an image. Justice binds because it reflects a Judge whose character does not change. Beauty summons because it is the echo of a greater splendor. And history keeps its appointments because the Author stepped onto the stage—was seen, touched, crucified, and raised.

This does not reduce life to a theorem. It raises reason to its proper dignity. Reason is not a cage for faith; it is the lamp that leads us to the door. We have come as far as reason can bring us without ceasing to be reason. To go further is not to abandon the mind but to fulfill its search with the truth it was made to find.

What the Evidence Shows

- The order of nature is not an accident of chaos but the signature of a Mind.

- The moral law is not a fashion of tribes but the imprint of a Lawgiver.
- The milestones of history form a pattern too precise to be luck; prophecy meets event.
- The pursuits we most cherish—truth, goodness, beauty—are not inventions; they are windows through which the same light falls.

What the Evidence Cannot Do

- It cannot choose for you.
- It cannot love for you.
- It cannot carry you the last few steps that only a willing heart can walk.

The Illusion of Neutrality

It is tempting to linger at a safe distance—interested, but uncommitted. Yet, neutrality in the face of convergence is not caution; it is decision. If the map is true and the shore is in sight, refusing to steer is a choice to drift. If the light is on and you close your eyes, you have still chosen darkness. Unreasonable doubt can purify; it can burn away pretense and force us to seek what is real. But there is a point at which doubt ceases to be honest inquiry and becomes evasion. Unreasonable doubt is the refusal to accept a conclusion because we dislike the cost of its truth. It is the mind using its brilliance to hide from the heart's responsibility.

The Cost of Truth

Every love has a cost. To say "yes" to the truth is to say "no" to a thousand lesser rulers. To bow to the God who is there is to resign the little throne we build for ourselves. But the cost of truth is the price of freedom, and the surrender of pride is the recovery of self. The cross is not merely the place where our debt was paid; it is the door through which we become our truest selves.

The Shape of the Next Step

We will not ask you to forget the mind to make a leap. We will ask you to honor the mind enough to follow it to its end—and then to let love do what reason has prepared.

***

Part 8 is not an argument; it is a summons. It is the moment when the evidence you have grasped with your intellect speaks to your conscience and asks for your answer. What awaits beyond the threshold is this: no one who comes to the truth comes to a cold proposition. You come to a Person. You will not meet an abstraction but the One in whom truth is alive. The map we abandoned lies open again. The guardrails we dismissed are seen for what they are—mercy in wood and steel. And the story that began with dust draws near to the promise of the divine: not that we escape being human but that we become fully human in the light of God's love. Stand here for a moment. Feel the weight of the journey you have made: the questions you have asked, the realities you have faced, the answers that have gathered around you like witnesses.

Part 8 will not ask you for perfect knowledge; it will ask you for courage. The road ahead is not a retreat from reason but a step into reality—a step from convergence to commitment, from seeing to saying "yes." The last turn is before you. When you make it, you will not be losing yourself. You will be finding your way home.

PART 8

The Unavoidable Decision

Chapter 1

From Convergence to Commitment

You have seen enough to know that neutrality is no longer honest. The roads we traced—meaning, justice, knowledge, beauty; the pattern of history; the order of the cosmos; the witness of conscience—have gathered into a single horizon. Reason has not been sidelined. It has done its noble work. Now it stands beside you at the threshold and says, "Go on." This is not a demand to feel something on command. It is a call to do what minds were made to do when they recognize the truth: to assent, to trust, to step. The gospel is not merely true in the abstract; it is true in the personal. It asks not just, "Do you agree?" but, "Will you come?"

The Honesty Test

Intellectual integrity is not only the courage to doubt; it is the courage to finish doubt's journey. Unreasonable doubt refuses to land because landing has a cost. Honest doubt accepts the cost and lands where the evidence leads. If the map is right, the next move is not more maps; it is travel.

The Anatomy of a Yes

Saying yes to Christ is not a leap into fog. It is a series of clear moves:

- *Confession*—Naming reality as it is, God is holy; I am not. I have loved lesser things as though they were ultimate.
- *Repentance*—Turning the will, I renounce those lesser rulers and return to the One worthy of rule.
- *Trust*—Placing confidence in the Person and work of Jesus: his cross bears my debt; his resurrection opens my life.
- *Surrender*—Yielding the throne, I entrust my mind, my loves, my future to the God who is Truth and Love. This is not self-erasure; it is self-recovery. The smaller throne we abandon is the prison we mistook for a kingdom.

Count the Cost—and the Other Cost

There is a cost to allegiance: you will unlearn some loves, relearn others, and accept disciplines that free you. But there is also a cost to refusal: drift instead of direction, appetite in place of purpose, brilliance without wisdom, achievement without peace. One cost purchases freedom; the other purchases a faster drift.

The Prayer Jesus Taught—The Lord's Prayer

Pray in the very words Jesus gave—sufficient for every circumstance, simple and inexhaustible in meaning:

> Our Father which art in heaven, Hallowed be thy name. Thy kingdom come. Thy will be done in earth, as it is in heaven. Give us this day our daily bread. And forgive us our debts, as we forgive our debtors. And lead us not into temptation, but deliver us from evil: For thine is the kingdom, and the power, and the glory, for ever. Amen.

How This Prayer Meets Every Circumstance

- "Father"—Identity and Intimacy: You are wanted, known, and loved.
- "Hallowed be thy name"—Worship: Reality starts with God's worth, not our wants.
- "Thy kingdom come"—Allegiance: His reign, not our rule, is the hope of the world.
- "Thy will be done"—Surrender and Guidance: Obedience before outcomes.
- "Daily bread"—Provision: God cares for bodily needs as well as souls.
- "Forgive us"—Mercy Received: Grace is stronger than our guilt.
- "As we forgive"—Mercy Given: Community is healed by shared grace.
- "Lead us not . . . deliver us"—Protection: Moral resilience and rescue from evil.
- "For thine is the kingdom"—Hope and Assurance: History is in faithful hands.

First Steps on Solid Ground

- *Scripture with a Scholar's Patience*—Read the Gospels slowly; note questions; seek answers.
- *Prayer with a Child's Candor*—Make it short, honest, and daily: ask, thank, confess, and request.
- *Community with Integrity*—Gather with Christians who love truth and love people. Avoid pretense; pursue accountability.
- *Service with Justice and Mercy*—Put your hands where your convictions are: protect the vulnerable, tell the truth, keep your promises.

- *Study that Worships*—Let your craft (science, art, business, care) become consecrated curiosity offered to God.

If You Are Not Ready

Honor the search. Refuse cynicism. Read the Gospels end-to-end. Ask the hardest questions you have been avoiding. Speak with people who will not flatter your doubts. Do not confuse postponement with wisdom. The tide always pulls; drift is never neutral.

The Joy on the Other Side of Yes

The aim is not mere survival but life—life with God, life made whole. The mind finds a home for truth. The conscience finds clean air. Love steadies. Work takes on meaning. Sorrow is met, not mocked. And hope becomes more than optimism: it becomes the expectation of a kingdom where justice and mercy are one. You are standing at the last turn before home. You do not walk alone. The One who called you through the evidence will meet you in the step itself. Say yes—and begin.

Chapter 2

The Courage to Say Yes

You are closer than you think. The distance between knowing and living is not measured in miles but in courage. We have not asked you to silence reason or to manufacture a feeling. We have asked you to honor what you already see and to take the step that sight requires. The step is not theatrical. It is simple, exact, and costly—in the same way truth is costly and love is exact. This chapter is a hand on your shoulder. If part 7 gathered the witnesses and part 8, chapter 1 opened the door, this chapter helps your feet move. It names the common fears, sets a rule of life that braids head and heart, and calls you to a public yes—not to impress anyone but to align your whole being with the truth you have found.

The Obstacles That Feel Like Walls

- *Fear of Change*—You are not asked to become less yourself but more truly yourself. God does not erase personality; he purifies it. What is false burns; what is true shines.
- *The Weight of the Past*—Guilt says, "I am what I have done." The gospel answers, "You are what Christ has done." Repentance is not denial; it is a truthful turning. Mercy is not amnesia; it is a new beginning with your eyes open.

- *Intellectual Pride*—Pride whispers that to bow is to betray the mind. In reality, pride is the betrayal; humility is the mind's highest act—assent to reality as it is. The greatest thinkers did not shrink when truth demanded homage—they stood taller.
- *Social Pressure*—Some will misunderstand your yes. Let them. You are not leaving the world; you are learning to love it truly. The first courage will give birth to many courages.

A Rule of Life for New Clarity (Thirty Days)

- *Daily*—Read the Lord's Prayer slowly, line by line. Read one chapter of a Gospel. Pray honestly for five minutes: ask, thank, confess, request. Keep a short list of people to forgive and people to serve.
- *Weekly*—Gather with Christians who love truth and love people. Receive Scripture and communion if available. Speak with someone who will tell you the truth about yourself in love.
- *Monthly*—Choose one act of costly service (time, talent, or treasure) that benefits those who cannot repay you. Bring a question that troubled you this month to a trusted pastor or thoughtful believer and seek a real answer.
- *Always*—Tell the truth. Keep your promises. Refuse contempt. Practice hidden kindness. These acts are small altars on which pride dies and love survives.

How to Make Your Yes Public (and Keep It)

Confession is personal; discipleship is public. Consider marking your commitment in ways that bind you to a community and a path: baptism (if you have not been baptized), joining a healthy church, serving on a team, and setting an appointment with a mentor who will ask you hard questions kindly. Public does not mean performative. It means accountable.

How the Lord's Prayer Stabilizes the Will

Repeat the prayer Jesus taught as the spine of your days. When fear rises: "Our Father." When pride rises: "Hallowed be thy name." When confusion rises: "Thy kingdom come, thy will be done." When want rises: "Give us this day our daily bread." When shame rises: "Forgive us our debts." When bitterness rises: "As we forgive our debtors." When temptation rises: "Lead us not . . . deliver us." When despair rises: "For thine is the kingdom and the power and the glory for ever."

A Short Litany for Courage

- Truth before comfort.
- Holiness before popularity.
- Love before victory.
- Obedience before outcomes.
- Jesus before everything.

If you said yes long ago (and grew tired), come home. Weariness is not failure; wandering is not final. Begin again today. Read Ps 51 aloud. Pray the Lord's Prayer. Tell someone you trust where you've lost heart. Serve someone who cannot repay you. Small obediences break large stagnations.

If you are still not ready, then honor the search with integrity. Read the Gospel of John end to end. Keep a written list of questions and pursue real answers. Sit with Christians who are thoughtful and unafraid. Ask God directly, "If You are there, make me honest and show me what I am resisting." Do not confuse delay with depth. Drift is never neutral.

Part 8: The Unavoidable Decision

The Moment of Courage

There is a moment in every honest life when truth demands a name and love demands a yes. Let today be that moment. Your yes will not make you perfect; it will make you his. It will not end struggle; it will end aimlessness. It will not answer every question; it will anchor every question in Someone who does not change. Say yes. Then begin the next right thing—read, pray, gather, serve, tell the truth, forgive, persevere. The road that brought you here will not vanish when you step forward. It will widen.

And the One who drew you with reason will hold you with love.

Bibliography

Aharoni, Yohanan, and Michael Avi-Yonah. *The Macmillan Bible Atlas.* 3rd ed. New York: Macmillan, 1993.

Amnesty International. "India 2024." https://www.amnesty.org/en/location/asia-and-the-pacific/south-asia/india/report-india/.

Aquinas, Thomas. *Summa Theologiae.* Part I. Translated by the Fathers of the English Dominican Province. New York: Benziger Brothers, 1947.

Archer, Gleason L. *A Survey of Old Testament Introduction.* Chicago: Moody, 1994.

Armstrong, Karen. *Islam: A Short History.* New York: Modern Library, 2000.

———. *Muhammad: A Prophet for Our Time.* New York: HarperOne, 2006.

Bajoria, Jayshree. "'They Say We're Dirty': Denying an Education to India's Marginalized." Human Rights Watch, Apr. 22, 2014. https://www.hrw.org/report/2014/04/22/they-say-were-dirty/denying-education-indias-marginalized.

Barbour, Stephanie, et al. "Hidden Apartheid: Caste Discrimination Against India's 'Untouchables.'" Human Rights Watch, Feb. 12, 2007. https://www.hrw.org/report/2007/02/12/hidden-apartheid/caste-discrimination-against-indias-untouchables.

Barnes, Luke A. "The Fine-Tuning of the Universe for Intelligent Life." *Publications of the Astronomical Society of Australia* 29.4 (2012) 529–64.

BBC News. "China's Pre-Christmas Crackdown Raises Alarm." Dec. 17, 2018. https://www.bbc.com/news/world-asia-china-46588650.

Biran, Avraham, and Joseph Naveh. "An Aramaic Stele Fragment from Tel Dan." *Israel Exploration Journal* 43.2–3 (1993) 81–98.

———. "The Tel Dan Inscription: A New Fragment." *Israel Exploration Journal* 45.1 (1995) 1–18.

Belmonte, Kevin. *William Wilberforce: A Hero for Humanity.* Grand Rapids: Zondervan, 2007.

Bergunder, Michael. *The South Indian Pentecostal Movement in the Twentieth Century.* Grand Rapids: Eerdmans, 2008.

Bethge, Eberhard. *Dietrich Bonhoeffer: A Biography.* Revised ed. Minneapolis: Fortress, 2000.

Bibliography

Blaising, Craig A., and Darrell L. Bock. *Dispensationalism, Israel and the Church: The Search for Definition*. Grand Rapids: Zondervan, 1992.

Blomberg, Craig L. *The Historical Reliability of the Gospels*. Downers Grove, IL: IVP Academic, 2007.

Bonhoeffer, Dietrich. *Letters and Papers from Prison*. Edited by Eberhard Bethge. New York: Touchstone, 1997.

Borde, Arvind, et al. "Inflationary Spacetimes Are Not Past-Eternal." *Physical Review Letters* 90 (2003) 151301. https://doi.org/10.1103/PhysRevLett.90.151301.

Boyle, Robert. *The Works of Robert Boyle*. Edited by Michael Hunter and Edward B. Davis. 14 vols. London: Pickering & Chatto, 1999–2000.

Bruce, F. F. *The Books and the Parchments*. Revised ed. Westwood, NJ: Revell, 1963.

Burke, Edmund. *A Philosophical Enquiry into the Origin of Our Ideas of the Sublime and Beautiful*. Edited by Adam Phillips. Oxford: Oxford University Press, 1990.

Burkert, Walter. *Ancient Mystery Cults*. Cambridge, MA: Harvard University Press, 1987.

Burton, John. *The Collection of the Qur'an*. Cambridge: Cambridge University Press, 1977.

Casali, Adenauer G., et al. "A Theoretically Based Index of Consciousness Independent of Sensory Processing and Behavior." *Science Translational Medicine* 5.198 (2013) 105.

Caspar, Max. *Kepler*. New York: Dover, 1993.

Chalmers, David J. *The Conscious Mind: In Search of a Fundamental Theory*. New York: Oxford University Press, 1996.

———. "Facing Up to the Problem of Consciousness." *Journal of Consciousness Studies* 2.3 (1995) 200–219.

Charlesworth, James H. *Jesus and Archaeology*. Grand Rapids: Eerdmans, 2006.

Citizens for Justice and Peace. "Everyday Atrocity: How Caste Violence Became India's New Normal." Aug. 23, 2025. https://cjp.org.in/everyday-atrocity-how-caste-violence-became-indias-new-normal/.

Cook, Michael. *The Koran: A Very Short Introduction*. Oxford: Oxford University Press, 2000.

Crick, Francis. *What Mad Pursuit: A Personal View of Scientific Discovery*. New York: Basic Books, 1988.

Dalley, Stephanie. *Myths from Mesopotamia*. Oxford: Oxford University Press, 2000.

Das, Maitreyi Bordia, and Soumya Kapoor Mehta. "Poverty and Social Exclusion in India: Dalits." The World Bank Group, 2012. https://openknowledge.worldbank.org/server/api/core/bitstreams/7504658a-35d3-5676-99fb-dc5c60e8c268/content.

Davies, Paul. *The Goldilocks Enigma: Why Is the Universe Just Right for Life?* London: Allen Lane, 2006.

Bibliography

Dawkins, Richard. *The Blind Watchmaker: Why the Evidence of Evolution Reveals a Universe Without Design*. New York: Norton, 1986.

Descartes, René. *Meditations on First Philosophy*. Translated by John Cottingham. Cambridge: Cambridge University Press, 2017.

DeVotta, Neil. "Buddhist Nationalism and Ethnic Conflict in Sri Lanka." *Journal of Asian Studies* 73.2 (2014) 453–73.

Dirac, P. A. M. *Directions in Physics*. Hoboken, NJ: Wiley & Sons, 1978.

Dirks, Nicholas B. *Castes of Mind: Colonialism and the Making of Modern India*. Princeton: Princeton University Press, 2001.

Donner, Fred M. *Muhammad and the Believers: At the Origins of Islam*. Cambridge, MA: Harvard University Press, 2010.

Dunn, James D. G. *Jesus Remembered*. Grand Rapids: Eerdmans, 2003.

Ehrman, Bart D. *Did Jesus Exist? The Historical Argument for Jesus of Nazareth*. New York: HarperOne, 2012.

Ehrman, Bart D., and Daniel B. Wallace. "The Textual Reliability of the New Testament: A Dialogue." In *The Reliability of the New Testament*, edited by Robert B. Stewart, 13–60. Minneapolis: Fortress, 2011.

Einstein, Albert. *Out of My Later Years*. New York: Philosophical Library, 1950.

Esposito, John L. *Islam: The Straight Path*. 4th ed. New York: Oxford University Press, 2016.

Evans, Craig A. *Jesus and His World: The Archaeological Evidence*. Louisville: Westminster John Knox, 2012.

Finocchiaro, Maurice A. *The Galileo Affair: A Documentary History*. Berkeley: University of California Press, 1989.

Flood, Gavin. *An Introduction to Hinduism*. Cambridge: Cambridge University Press, 1996.

Force, James, and Richard Popkin, eds. *The Books of Nature and Scripture: Recent Essays on Natural Philosophy, Theology, and Biblical Criticism in the Netherlands of Spinoza's Time*. Dordrecht, NL: Kluwer, 1994.

Fredriksen, Paula. *Jesus of Nazareth, King of the Jews*. New York: Vintage, 2000.

Galilei, Galileo. "Letter to the Grand Duchess Christina." In *Discoveries and Opinions of Galileo*, translated by Stillman Drake, 145–216. New York: Anchor, 1957.

Global Forum of Communities Discriminated on Work and Descent (GFoD). "Communities Discriminated on Work and Descent in India: India Report 2023–2024." https://globalforumcdwd.org/wp-content/uploads/2024/02/Indian-Report.pdf.

The Guardian. "China Jails Underground Pastor Wang Yi for Nine Years for Inciting Subversion." Dec. 30, 2019. https://www.theguardian.com/law/2019/dec/30/china-jails-underground-pastor-wang-yi-for-nine-years-for-inciting-subversion.

Gombrich, Richard. *Theravada Buddhism: A Social History from Ancient Benares to Modern Colombo*. London: Routledge, 1988.

Habermas, Gary R. "1 Corinthians 15:3–7: The Earliest Gospel Tradition." *Journal for the Study of the Historical Jesus* 5.2 (2007) 167–87.

Bibliography

Habermas, Jürgen. *An Awareness of What Is Missing: Faith and Reason in a Post-Secular Age*. Cambridge, UK: Polity, 2010.

Hague, William. *William Wilberforce: The Life of the Great Anti-Slave Trade Campaigner*. London: HarperCollins, 2007.

Hardy, G. H. *A Mathematician's Apology*. Cambridge: Cambridge University Press, 1940.

Hawking, Stephen, and Leonard Mlodinow. *The Grand Design*. New York: Bantam, 2010.

Hawking, Stephen, and Roger Penrose. *The Nature of Space and Time*. Princeton, NJ: Princeton University Press, 1996.

Hochschild, Adam. *Bury the Chains: Prophets and Rebels in the Fight to Free an Empire's Slaves*. Boston: Houghton Mifflin, 2005.

Holland, Tom. *Dominion: How the Christian Revolution Remade the World*. New York: Basic Books, 2019.

Hoyle, Fred. "The Universe: Past and Present Reflections." *Engineering and Science* 45.3 (1981) 8–12.

Human Rights Watch. "'All You Can Do Is Pray': Crimes Against Humanity and Ethnic Cleansing of Rohingya Muslims in Burma's Arakan State." HRW Report, Apr. 22, 2013. https://www.hrw.org/report/2013/04/22/all-you-can-do-pray/crimes-against-humanity-and-ethnic-cleansing-rohingya-muslims.

Hunter, Michael. *Boyle: Between God and Science*. New Haven, CT: Yale University Press, 2009.

International Christian Concern. "Imprisoned Chinese Pastor's Church Vows to Keep Fighting." Jan. 8, 2020. https://persecution.org/2020/01/08/imprisoned-chinese-pastors-church-vows-to-keep-fighting/.

International Crisis Group. "The Dark Side of Transition: Violence Against Muslims in Myanmar." ICG Asia Report No. 251, Oct. 1, 2013. https://www.crisisgroup.org/asia-pacific/myanmar/251-dark-side-transition-violence-against-muslims-myanmar.

International Dalit Solidarity Network. "Dalit Women." https://idsn.org/key-issues/dalit-women/.

Ishaq, Ibn. *Sirat Rasul Allah* [The Life of Muhammad]. Translated by A. Guillaume. Oxford: Oxford University Press, 1955.

Jodhka, Surinder S. *Caste in Contemporary India*. London: Routledge, 2015.

Josephus, Flavius. *Jewish Antiquities*. In *Josephus: The Essential Writings*, translated by Paul L. Maier, 19–280. Grand Rapids: Kregel, 1990.

Kaiser, Walter C., Jr. *The Messiah in the Old Testament*. Grand Rapids: Zondervan, 1995.

Kauffman, Stuart. *Origins of Order: Self-Organization and Selection in Evolution*. New York: Oxford University Press, 1993.

Kennedy, Hugh. *The Great Arab Conquests: How the Spread of Islam Shaped the World We Live In*. Philadelphia: Da Capo, 2007.

Keown, Damien. *Buddhism: A Very Short Introduction*. Oxford: Oxford University Press, 2013.

Bibliography

Kepler, Johannes. *The Harmonies of the World*. Translated by E. J. Aiton, et al. Philadelphia: American Philosophical Society, 1997.

Kim, Sebastian C. H., and Kirsteen Kim. *A History of Korean Christianity in India*. Cambridge: Cambridge University Press, 2014.

Krauss, Lawrence M. *A Universe from Nothing: Why Is There Something Rather Than Nothing*. New York: Atria, 2012.

Lewis, C. S. *The Abolition of Man*. New York: HarperOne, 2001.

Lüdemann, Gerd. *The Resurrection of Christ: A Historical Inquiry*. Amherst, NY: Prometheus, 2004.

MacIntyre, Alasdair. *After Virtue: A Study in Moral Theory*. Notre Dame: University of Notre Dame Press, 1981.

McDermott, Gerald R., ed. *Understanding the Jewish Roots of Christianity: Biblical, Theological, and Historical Essays*. Nashville: B&H Academic, 2021.

McDowell, Josh. *Evidence That Demands a Verdict*. Updated ed. Nashville: Thomas Nelson, 2017.

McRay, John. *Archaeology and the New Testament*. Grand Rapids: Baker Academic, 1991.

Metaxas, Eric. *Bonhoeffer: Pastor, Martyr, Prophet, Spy*. Nashville: Thomas Nelson, 2010.

Metzger, Bruce M., and Bart D. Ehrman. *The Text of the New Testament: Its Transmission, Corruption, and Restoration*. 4th ed. New York: Oxford University Press, 2005.

Monod, Jacques. *Chance and Necessity: Essay on the Natural Philosophy of Modern Biology*. New York: Vintage, 1972.

Mustafa al-Azami, Muhammad. *The History of the Qur'anic Text: From Revelation to Compilation*. 2nd ed. Riyadh, SA: Azami, 2003.

Nandakumar, Prathima. "Lives, Buried: Untouchability Persists in India, Across Villages and Cities." *The Week*, Apr. 20, 2025. https://www.theweek.in/theweek/cover/2025/04/12/despite-being-banned-by-the-constitution-untouchability-persists-in-india-across-villages-and-cities.html.

Newton, Isaac. *The Principia: Mathematical Principles of Natural Philosophy*. Translated by Andrew Motte. Berkeley: University of California Press, 1962.

Nietzsche, Friedrich. *On the Genealogy of Morals*. Translated by Walter Kaufmann and R. J. Hollingdale. New York: Vintage, 1989.

Penrose, Roger. *The Road to Reality: A Complete Guide to the Laws of the Universe*. London: Jonathan Cape, 2004.

Peters, F. E. *Islam: A Guide for Jews and Christians*. Princeton: Princeton University Press, 2003.

Planck Collaboration. "Planck 2018 Results. VI. Cosmological Parameters." *Astronomy & Astrophysics* 641 (2020) A6.

Plato. *Five Dialogues: Euthyphro, Apology, Crito, Meno, Phaedo*. 2nd ed. Translated by G. M. A. Grube. Indianapolis: Hackett, 2002.

Bibliography

Prigogine, Ilya. *Order Out of Chaos: Man's New Dialogue with Nature.* New York: Bantam, 1984.

Rahula, Walpola. *What the Buddha Taught.* New York: Grove, 1974.

Rees, Martin. *Just Six Numbers: The Deep Forces That Shape the Universe.* London: Weidenfeld & Nicolson, 1999.

Reynolds, Gabriel Said, ed. *The Qur'an in Its Historical Context.* London: Routledge, 2008.

Robinson, Richard H., and Willard L. Johnson. *The Buddhist Religion: A Historical Introduction.* Belmont, CA: Wadsworth, 1997.

Robinson, Rowena. *Christians of India.* Thousand Oaks, CA: Sage, 2003.

Rydelnik, Michael. *The Messianic Hope: Is the Hebrew Bible Really Messianic?* Nashville: B&H Academic, 2010.

Sagan, Carl. *Cosmos.* New York: Random House, 1980.

Sanders, E. P. *The Historical Figure of Jesus.* London: Penguin, 1993.

Śaṅkara, Sri. *Brahma-Sūtras.* Translated by Swami Vireswarananda. Calcutta: Advaita Ashrama, 1936.

Sarasso, Simone, et al. "Consciousness and Complexity During Unresponsiveness Induced by Propofol, Xenon, and Ketamine." *Current Biology* 25.23 (2015) 3099–105.

Sartre, Jean-Paul. *Existentialism Is a Humanism.* Translated by Carol Macomber. New Haven, CT: Yale University Press, 2007.

Selvaraj, Aruldoss, and Marianathan Chinnasamy. "Towards a New Dawn with Dalit Empowerment." Jesuits, July 13, 2020. https://www.jesuits.global/2020/07/13/towards-a-new-dawn-with-dalit-empowerment/.

Shanks, Hershel. "The Pool of Siloam Has Been Found." *Biblical Archaeology Review* 31.6 (2005) 16–23.

Shermer, Michael. *Why Darwin Matters: The Case Against Intelligent Design.* New York: Times Books, 2006.

Spiro, Melford E. *Buddhism and Society: A Great Tradition and Its Burmese Vicissitudes.* Berkeley: University of California Press, 1982.

Srinivas, M. N. *Social Change in Modern India.* Berkeley: University of California Press, 1966.

Tacitus. *The Annals: The Reigns of Tiberius, Claudius, and Nero.* Translated J. C. Yardley. Oxford: Oxford University Press, 2008.

Tambiah, Stanley J. *Buddhism Betrayed? Religion, Politics, and Violence in Sri Lanka.* Chicago: University of Chicago Press, 1992.

Tononi, Giulio. "Consciousness as Integrated Information: A Provisional Manifesto." *Biological Bulletin* 215.3 (2008) 216–42.

———. "An Information Integration Theory of Consciousness." *BMC Neuroscience* 5.42 (2004) 1–22.

Tononi, Giulio, and Christof Koch. "Consciousness: Here, There and Everywhere?" *Philosophical Transactions of the Royal Society* B.370 (2015) 20140167.

United Nations. "Declaration on the Elimination of All Forms of Intolerance and of Discrimination Based on Religion or Belief." General Assembly

Bibliography

Resolution 36/55, Nov. 25, 1981. https://www.ohchr.org/en/instruments-mechanisms/instruments/declaration-elimination-all-forms-intolerance-and-discrimination.

US Commission on International Religious Freedom (USCIRF). "Annual Report 2020." Apr. 2020. https://www.uscirf.gov/sites/default/files/USCIRF%202020%20Annual%20Report_42720_new_0.pdf.

Vilenkin, Alexander. *Many Worlds in One: The Search for Other Universes.* New York: Hill and Wang, 2006.

Walton, Matthew J. *Buddhism, Politics and Political Thought in Myanmar.* Cambridge: Cambridge University Press, 2016.

Wang, Yi. "My Declaration of Faithful Disobedience." China Partnership, Dec. 12, 2018. Translated by Amy Pinkall, Brent Pinkall, and China Partnership Translation Team. https://chinapartnership.org/blog/2018/12/my-declaration-of-faithful-disobedience/.

Weinberg, Steven. *Dreams of a Final Theory: The Scientist's Search for the Ultimate Laws of Nature.* New York: Vintage, 1993.

Wigner, Eugene P. "The Unreasonable Effectiveness of Mathematics in the Natural Sciences." *Communications on Pure and Applied Mathematics* 13.1 (1960) 1–14.

Wilberforce, William. *A Practical View of Christianity.* London: T. Cadell, 1797.

World Vision India. "Child Wellbeing Report 2019." https://www.wvi.org/sites/default/files/2019-11/India-Child-Wellbeing-Report-Web.pdf.

Wright, N. T. *Jesus and the Victory of God.* Minneapolis: Fortress, 1996.

www.ingramcontent.com/pod-product-compliance
Lightning Source LLC
Chambersburg PA
CBHW060601230426
43670CB00011B/1917